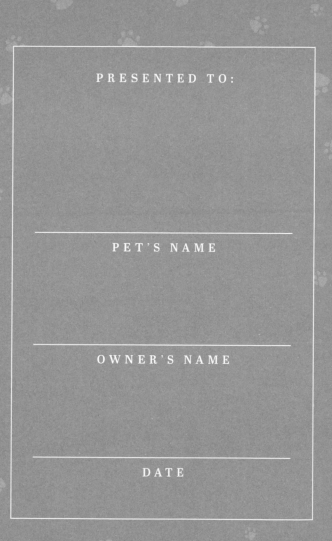

PRESENTED TO:

_____

PET'S NAME

_____

OWNER'S NAME

_____

DATE

Pawverbs for a Dog Lover's Heart

PAWVERBS
~ FOR A ~
DOG LOVER'S HEART

Inspiring Stories of Friendship, Fun, and Faithfulness

JENNIFER MARSHALL BLEAKLEY

The Tyndale nonfiction imprint

Visit Tyndale online at tyndale.com.

Visit Tyndale Momentum online at tyndalemomentum.com.

TYNDALE, Tyndale's quill logo, *Tyndale Momentum*, and the Tyndale Momentum logo are registered trademarks of Tyndale House Ministries. Tyndale Momentum is the nonfiction imprint of Tyndale House Publishers, Carol Stream, Illinois.

Pawverbs for a Dog Lover's Heart: Inspiring Stories of Friendship, Fun, and Faithfulness

Some of the stories were previously published in *Pawverbs: 100 Inspirations to Delight an Animal Lover's Heart* by Tyndale House Publishers in 2020 under the ISBN 978-1-4964-4105-8. First printing by Tyndale House Publishers in 2020.

Cover photograph of dog by Jack Brind on Unsplash.

The photograph of the author with her dog, Gracie, copyright © 2019 Greenflash Productions Photography. All rights reserved.

Designed by Ron C. Kaufmann

Edited by Bonne Steffen

Published in association with Jessica Kirkland and the literary agency of Kirkland Media Management, LLC.

For information about special discounts for bulk purchases, please contact Tyndale House Publishers at csresponse@tyndale.com, or call 1-855-277-9400.

ISBN 978-1-4964-4727-2

Printed in China

27	26	25	24	23	22	21
10	9	8	7	6	5	4

For Aunt Judy.
Thank you for getting me my first dog
and for being one of my best friends.

INTRODUCTION

EVERYWHERE I LOOK THESE DAYS, it seems there is a picture, story, article, or post about a dog. The world is finally understanding what we dog lovers have always known: Dogs make the world a better place. And if we let them, they have much to teach us about life, about ourselves, and even about God.

I think that one of God's greatest kindnesses to mankind was giving us dogs. Canine companions are quick to forgive, always willing to play, and content to just sit with us. They provide us with living, breathing safe places to which we can retreat. These loyal friends love us unconditionally and ultimately point us to God, who is the embodiment of perfect friendship and love.

Ironically, I was afraid of dogs when I was a child, as I share in "Hi, Donnie," the first story in this book. Although I didn't have a dog to call my own until I was married, many members of my family had wonderful dogs who enriched my life. Dogs have taught me powerful lessons about contentment, speaking up for myself, not taking myself too seriously, the importance of making time for play, and the power of being present with others.

The more I have observed my dogs—and the dogs I've been blessed to

know—the more I've learned from them. Not just life lessons, but spiritual lessons too, glimpses of the divine hiding in the ordinary. In fact, uncovering meaningful moments in the midst of everyday life actually motivated me to write this book. My goal was to showcase how our canine friends teach us and point us to truth and hope.

Pawverbs for a Dog Lover's Heart is a collection of dog stories, each based on a real dog and highlighting a principle or lesson found in the book of Proverbs. Several of the stories are about my own dogs throughout the years—including my current Golden retriever, Gracie. Most, however, were submitted by friends, family, coworkers, and even strangers who now feel like family. Some stories took place a long time ago and were written from memories and recollections, with names and identifying details changed for privacy, and a few timelines have been adjusted for a more cohesive story. But the heart and integrity of the stories are all based on true events.

At the end of each story, you will find a "Paws & Ponder" and a "Paws & Pray" feature to prompt you to go deeper into the story and see a spiritual truth that might impact your own heart.

My ultimate prayer is that within these pages you will find inspiration, laughter, healing, hope, and some new friends. And that you will be encouraged to "paws" and pay attention to the divine moments tucked inside of your ordinary days—divine moments that may just come running toward you with muddy paws.

Much love,

Jen

HI, DONNIE

Unrelenting disappointment leaves you heartsick,
but a sudden good break can turn life around.

PROVERBS 13:12, MSG

AS A YOUNG GIRL, Jen was terrified of dogs. Especially big dogs—like Donnie.

Her uncle Ron and aunt Nancy's German shepherd often accompanied them to family gatherings at Jen's grandparents' house. Jen's entire family loved Donnie. Her cousins often fought over who would get to play with him first.

But whenever five-year-old Jen caught sight of Donnie, she cowered behind her dad's leg, trembling. As much as Jen's relatives assured the little girl that Donnie wouldn't hurt her, she wasn't convinced. Consequently, her aunt and uncle always kept the shepherd outside and away from her. Their consideration helped, but it also magnified Jen's fear. She began to view Donnie as "the beast" who had to stay outside to keep him from attacking her.

Jen would watch longingly from the back door of the house as her cousins played with Donnie in their grandparents' backyard. They would play fetch and hide-and-seek, take turns shaking Donnie's paws, and ask him to roll over.

They all looked so happy, including Donnie.

Jen began to grow frustrated with herself. She loved her cousins and wanted to play with them. She didn't want to be scared anymore.

Yet every time she decided to face her fear and step outside, she pictured Donnie jumping up on her like he did to her cousin Mike. Or she heard Donnie's deep, throaty bark and slunk back down into the sofa cushions.

During one visit, Jen was tired of being cooped up inside and missing out on the fun.

She opened the back door and looked out on the porch where her grand-daddy was slicing a watermelon. Uncle Ron was sitting beside him, with Donnie lying at his feet.

When Uncle Ron spotted Jen, he stood up and grabbed Donnie's collar. "I'll take him inside," he offered.

"It's okay," Jen whispered.

"Donnie, sit," Uncle Ron said.

She eyed the big dog. His mouth was open, and his tongue was hanging out. His ears were raised, and his head was cocked to the side as if he were studying her. He sat completely still.

Jen began to inch her way forward on the porch. Once she reached Donnie, she cautiously placed her right hand on the top of his head.

"Hi, Donnie," she said, timidly smiling.

As if sensing the importance of the moment, Donnie lay down, rolled over, and offered her his belly.

"Well, I'll be," Jen heard her granddaddy say.

Jen knelt down and rubbed Donnie's belly—tentatively at first and then with more confidence. Within minutes, her fear disappeared.

From that time on, Donnie continued his boisterous play with Jen's cousins, but he was always gentle with Jen. Even in her five-year-old mind, she grasped lifelong lessons from him—about patience, not judging others based on their appearance, and what true friendship looked like.

PAWS & PONDER...

Are you struggling with a fear today? Lay it before your heavenly Father, and ask him to help you identify and take the first step to overcome that worry. Imagine the victory you will feel after walking through that fear, a victory you will share with the God who walks with you.

Paws & Pray

Father, thank you for being stronger than my fear. Give me courage to take the first step toward conquering my anxiety. I know I will not walk alone.

LOOK UP

Ears that hear and eyes that see—the LORD has made them both.

PROVERBS 20:12, NIV

AMBER CLEARED A PATH with her foot through a pile of dirty laundry so she could get to the back door. "Ow!" she cried as she stepped on a stray Lego.

"Mom!" her son and daughter yelled in unison. "Where are the goggles?"

"The new school year cannot start soon enough, Suzie Poo," Amber mumbled to their nine-week-old Australian shepherd–Queensland heeler mix, who wiggled anxiously in her arms.

"Hang on, girl. Let me open the door."

Once outside, Amber set the puppy on the grass and chanted, "Go potty," for what seemed like the eighty-seventh time that morning. Suzie's leash dangled from Amber's hand as she urged the puppy to do her business—hoping she would soon make the connection between the action and the appropriate location.

Amber glanced at her watch.

The kids need lunch before swim lessons.

Do I have bread?

What am I going to make for dinner?

Ugh, I forgot to put the clothes in the washer!

She jiggled the leash. "Hurry up, girl."

Amber felt a flood of stress engulf her. She loved being a mom. Loved having this time with her kids. Loved every gift God had given her.

But she was tired.

So tired.

She needed rest. And maybe a vacation in Maui.

Look up.

The words came as a whisper to her heart. Not audible to human ears, yet clear and authoritative to her soul.

And so Amber looked up.

The brilliant blue sky was awash with swirls of wispy clouds, creating lovely white patterns. A slight breeze caused the leaves in the maple tree to rustle and dance, and she laughed at two squirrels playing fast tag up another tree.

Amber inhaled deeply, driving the racing thoughts from her mind.

She took a deep breath, then another. Each time she felt as though she were inhaling God's rest and peace and exhaling her stress and worry. Her soul felt lighter.

With one last glance toward the heavens, Amber turned her attention back to Suzie Poo. "C'mon. Let's head inside." Her life as a mom didn't miraculously slow down and become manageable that summer—and she doubted it would for quite a while. But that day outside revealed an important truth to her: True rest can be found in little stolen moments with God.

That day, puppy training time turned from a necessary annoyance to a sacred time of rest with God. He opened Amber's eyes and ears to see and hear the wondrous beauty all around her.

And while she would gladly accept a Hawaiian vacation in the future, her stolen moments with God provided just what she needed in the moment.

PAWS & PONDER...

When have you felt closest to God? Where were you and what were you doing? Take a moment to "look up" today—to look above your circumstances and see a glimpse of the Creator. Use your eyes and ears to look at and listen closely to the things around you. Ask God to fill your soul with rest as you breathe in his presence.

Paws & Pray

Lord, my soul craves the rest only you can give. Would you lift my head so I can see well beyond my circumstances? Help me to see past the mundane in order to glimpse the divine.

Blessed is the one who finds wisdom,
and the one who gets understanding.

PROVERBS 3:13, ESV

GO LEFT

The prudent understand where they are going,
but fools deceive themselves.

PROVERBS 14:8

JUSTUS WAS ONLY A FEW months old the first time he saw a squirrel in his backyard climbing down a large oak tree.

The small yellow Lab, whose nose had been pressed to the ground as he explored his new surroundings, was startled by the sound of claws scratching against tree bark. Justus tilted his head, wagged his tail, and then he was off. Driven by both instinct and curiosity, Justus ran as fast as he could.

The squirrel stopped his descent, confident he was safe on the tree trunk several feet from the ground.

Justus barked and pawed the tree.

Desperate to play with this new and interesting friend, he play-bowed numerous times.

The squirrel was unimpressed and chattered noisily as he scampered farther up the trunk.

Confused and dejected, Justus stared at the tree for several minutes before lowering his nose and resuming his sniff patrol.

Day after day, the squirrel descended from its nest and Justus gave chase as it turned and scampered up the tree.

Squirrel quickly became Justus's favorite word. He would bark frantically at the mere mention of the creature who refused to come down for a proper hello.

As Justus grew from puppy to full-size dog, his interest in squirrels grew from curiosity to an all-out obsession.

And yet, much to his owner Will's amusement, no matter where in the yard a squirrel was, Justus always, without fail, ran straight to the oak tree in the middle of the backyard.

"Justus, squirrel!" Will would shout, pointing to a squirrel on the fence opposite the oak tree.

Justus would bark and paw at the door. He would see the squirrel to his left, balancing on the top of the fence. But the minute the door opened, Justus would make a hard right and run straight to the oak tree.

One day, hearing a squirrel's distinct chattering, Justus bounded out the door, took his hard right, and then let out a yelp. He limped to the tree.

No squirrel there.

Forlorn at not nabbing the elusive squirrel, he limped back inside.

Will took his squirrel hunter to the vet, who revealed that Justus's enthusiastic chase had resulted in a torn ACL.

"Oh, Justus," Will whispered in his Lab's ear while he was being prepped for surgery. "Next time go left."

Justus recovered from surgery and lived many more happy years. But never once did he turn left.

PAWS & PONDER . . .

Has your enthusiasm for something ever caused you to run ahead of God—or miss his leading altogether? Maybe it was a relationship or an opportunity you pursued despite the Holy Spirit prompting you not to. How did that situation turn out? How can you guard yourself from making a mistake when enthusiasm swells in your heart?

--- ✤ ---

Paws & Pray

Lord, so often I think I am going the right way in life, only to discover I've made a wrong turn. Help me to walk with you, Father—to go where you lead. Stop me from running ahead of your plans for me.

DID YOU HEAR SOMETHING?

The righteous choose their friends carefully,
but the way of the wicked leads them astray.

PROVERBS 12:26, NIV

AFTER LETTING THEIR TWO DOGS OUT—a gentle five-year-old rescued beagle mix named Delta and a year-old energetic Weimaraner named Wiley—Mark and Heather settled on the sofa to watch a movie. The couple had been looking forward to a date night at home. With their dogs securely playing in the fenced backyard, the house was finally quiet and movie night could begin.

Several minutes into the movie, as Heather reached for the bowl of popcorn sitting on the coffee table, she thought she heard a noise at the front door.

"Mark, did you hear that?"

"No," he said, pausing the movie.

She strained to listen. "Okay, now I don't hear anything."

"Probably just the surround sound," Mark said, clicking the remote to play the movie again.

Heather had eaten several handfuls of popcorn when she heard the noise again.

"I *know* I heard something now," she said, getting up.

Once again Mark paused the movie. This time they both heard the unmistakable sound of frantic scratching at the front door. Heather glanced through the front window.

"It's Delta and Wiley!" she exclaimed.

Mark opened the door, and their two dogs bounded in.

"How did you two get out?" Mark asked.

"And how long have you been standing there?" Heather continued the interrogation.

Clearly unwilling to share the details of their great backyard escape, Delta and Wiley plopped in front of the sofa and proceeded to sleep off their adventure.

The next day Mark discovered a freshly dug trench at the bottom of the fence—the perfect size for a Weimaraner to squeeze through.

Wiley!

The lanky dog with blue eyes was as striking looking as he was mischievous. Delta wanted nothing more than to obey and be rewarded for her obedience, while Wiley lived to break the rules.

Mark told Heather what he had found.

"Wiley, don't you lead Delta astray," Heather chided him.

At the sound of her name, Delta raised her head. Wiley simply rolled over.

"Keep your eye out for that one," Heather whispered to Delta. "And good job leading him back home."

Between his expert digging skills and a finicky gate lock, Wiley managed to escape several more times. But thankfully his wiser and more obedient companion Delta always convinced Wiley to follow her home—right to the front door.

PAWS & PONDER...

What makes a good friend? Why is it important to choose friends carefully? How can you be a good friend to someone today?

--- ❀ ---

Paws & Pray

Lord, thank you for the gift of friendship. I want to be more discerning about who I befriend. Teach me to be a valued friend to others—loving them as you do and as you love me.

Don't be impressed with your own wisdom. Instead,
fear the Lord and turn away from evil.

PROVERBS 3:7

PUGSLEY

A sluggard buries his hand in the dish;
he will not even bring it back to his mouth!

PROVERBS 19:24, NIV

SUSAN HAD NEVER SEEN HER DOG, Pugsley, look more pitiful than when she picked him up from the veterinary hospital after his dental cleaning. The seven-year-old pug trembled as the technician handed him to Susan.

"He did great," the tech said, "but I know he's ready to get out of here."

Susan offered an apologetic smile. "I don't know why he's so frightened to come here. You guys are great. He's just a big ol' scaredy-cat, aren't ya, boy?"

After a few parting instructions from the tech, Susan took Pugsley home, where he promptly fell asleep. After listening to him snore for several hours, Susan got up to prepare his dinner. The vet tech had suggested softening his kibble or giving him canned food for the next few days, in case his mouth was a little sore from the procedure. So Susan popped open a can of food and scooped it into Pugsley's ceramic bowl.

"Come, Pugsley, it's din-din time," she called.

The pug opened an eye but did not move a muscle.

"Pugsley," she tried again. "Come eat your dinner."

Pugsley got up, turned in a circle, then once again curled up in a ball on the sofa.

Susan carried the bowl of food to Pugsley and held it under his nose. He looked from his bowl to Susan, then back to his bowl. Finally, he lowered his head over his bowl and began to eat.

21

Susan felt guilty for letting her dog eat while lying on the furniture. *Just this once—because he's been through such an ordeal,* she assured herself.

The next day, when Pugsley again refused to come into the kitchen to eat, Susan tried to stand strong.

"Pugsley, you have to come *in here* to eat. Come here," she commanded.

Her dog stepped one paw into the kitchen and then lay down. Two big round eyes stared beseechingly at her.

"Oh, all right," Susan sighed. "At least you're in the kitchen."

She again brought his bowl to him, where he leisurely ate with his front half on the kitchen's tile floor and his back half on the family room carpet.

After four days of catering to her dog—including hand-feeding him—Susan realized her dog had become quite lazy and spoiled. At his last feeding, he didn't even lower his head to the bowl, but simply waited for Susan to bring the kibble to his mouth. She knew she needed to bring Pugsley back to reality. So the following day she poured a scoop of kibble into his food bowl and placed it next to his water bowl on the floor.

"Pugsley," she called out. "Dinner!"

Pugsley sashayed into the kitchen where he sat with his hind end on the carpet and his front paws on the tile.

"Oh no, you don't," Susan chided. "You are coming in here to eat today, mister."

Pugsley turned the full force of his sad puppy eyes on her, but Susan was resolved.

The standoff lasted several hours, during which time Susan completed a lengthy list of household chores, while Pugsley stared longingly at the food bowl lying ten feet away from him.

Finally, after his pleading looks and incessant whining went unanswered, the disgruntled pug sulked his way into the kitchen, lowered his head over his bowl, and surrendered to his hunger.

Twenty minutes later Susan laughed out loud as Pugsley sank to the floor with his head on his food bowl and fell sound asleep.

Susan shook her head as she carried the pug to his bed. "You silly dog. You may be a scaredy-cat and a lazybones, but I sure do love you."

PAWS & PONDER...

A one-time indulgence resulted in an unintended pattern for Susan and Pugsley. Have you ever experienced a similar result? How did you break the habit? Or maybe you are still stuck in that routine. If so, what steps can you take today to break free of the destructive pattern of laziness and/or overindulgence?

_____   🐾   _____

Paws & Pray

Lord, I love to be comfortable and content, but sometimes those things can become bad habits if I'm not careful. I sometimes opt to be lazy and self-indulgent when I should be doing the work you've given me to do. Help me to fight against those destructive patterns so I can live a full and purposeful life.

The fear of man lays a snare,
but whoever trusts in the Lord *is safe.*

6

LET'S GO, BULLET

The fear of man lays a snare,
but whoever trusts in the Lord is safe.

PROVERBS 29:25, ESV

ICE PELLETS STUNG SARAH'S FACE as she walked her year-old dog, Bullet, early one February morning. As the sleet increased, Sarah picked up speed, doing her best to avoid icy spots on the sidewalk.

"Only for you, Bullet. Only for you would I walk in the freezing cold before dawn." With her husband, Kory, away on business, and her workday full of meetings, Sarah knew Bullet needed to burn off some energy at the dog park before being left at home for the day.

When they arrived, they had the park to themselves. Sarah closed the gate behind her and unsnapped the leash from Bullet's collar. "Go on. Have fun," she said, watching him run around the inside perimeter of the enclosure. *You've made so much progress since we met you at the animal shelter, Bullet.*

Six months earlier, the Lab mix had bonded readily to Sarah, gladly accepting pets and belly rubs, but he was much more nervous around men.

Sarah had reached out to the animal shelter for more information. It had broken her heart to discover the horrific abuse her dog had suffered at the hands of his previous owner—a man with no patience for an exuberant puppy.

Sarah and Kory had worked hard to gain Bullet's trust. And while it had taken several months, Bullet was finally starting to let Kory hand him a treat. But Bullet still wouldn't come near Sarah's dad, who loved dogs and visited often.

"It's a work in progress," her dad would say, shrugging off Bullet's behavior. "I'll win him over one of these days."

This morning Bullet came bounding to Sarah—clearly wanting to play. She

25

glanced around. *Yes!* There was a tennis ball near the picnic tables. Bullet began jumping with anticipation, as Sarah placed the ball on the ground.

"Do you want it? You'd better start running," Sarah said playfully.

She swung her leg out to kick the ball and . . . slipped on a patch of black ice that had been hidden under the snow. Her feet flew out from under her as she fell over backward, instinctively putting her hands behind her to break her fall.

As she tried to get up, everything seemed to be spinning, and intense pain was shooting up and down her arms.

Something is wrong with my wrists. I can't make it home with Bullet. I can't hold his leash. I need to get help. She inched one hand slowly to her pocket and pulled out her phone. She could barely dial her parents' number.

Her dad said he was on his way.

Sarah managed to get to a picnic table, so exhausted and dizzy she could barely call Bullet's name. The reality of the situation made the pain worse.

How was she going to get Bullet to go to her dad and get him into the car?

Bullet sat several feet away from Sarah, head tilted, eyes fixed on her. Then he resumed his exploration of the park but kept a watchful eye on her.

And then her dad was there. He drove his SUV straight down the hill path and up to the dog park gate. When he got out of the car, Sarah watched helplessly. What would Bullet do?

Bullet looked at Sarah and seemed to sense that something was wrong. He began walking toward her dad. He stopped, lowered his head, and stayed still as Sarah's dad clipped a leash to Bullet's collar.

"Let's go, Bullet," he said. Immediately Bullet jumped in the backseat of the car.

"Told you he would come around," her dad said with a wink, as he came back and helped Sarah to the car.

And indeed Bullet did. As Sarah's broken wrists healed, so did Bullet's fear of Sarah's dad; they bonded deeply, eventually becoming the very best of friends.

PAWS & PONDER...

While Bullet's fear of men was understandable and justified, why could that fear have been a "snare" for him in this situation? What might have happened if Bullet hadn't trusted Sarah's father? Is it easy for you to shrug off what others think of you or what they can do to you? How does trusting in the Lord keep you safe?

_____   🐾   _____

Paws & Pray

Father God, help me to trust in you more and more each day. Sometimes it is difficult for me to remember that you are bigger and greater and stronger than my fears. Open my eyes to see the truth—that no one can harm my soul or take me away from you. Bolster my courage!

A GOOD NAME

A good name is more desirable than great riches;
to be esteemed is better than silver or gold.

PROVERBS 22:1, NIV

"DARCY!"

With one word—the name of her very best friend—the two-year-old Golden retriever named Gracie woke from a sound sleep.

"Want to see Darcy?" Jen, her human, asked, her voice rising an octave on the last syllable.

Gracie stood up, vigorously shook herself from nose to tail, then immediately broke into her "Darcy dance." She ran from window to window looking for her best canine friend. She pawed at the door. She spun in tight circles. She jumped at the knob on the back door, willing someone to take pity on her and open it.

Gracie simply could not wait to get to Darcy, the ten-year-old Portuguese water dog who lived across the street. The two had been friends since Gracie was a puppy and Darcy towered over her. Now the two dogs stood shoulder to shoulder. And although they differed in age and breed, the two had been best friends since they first sniffed each other more than two years ago.

"So, I take it you *do* want to see Darcy?" Jen teased.

Gracie barked her answer, scratching frantically at the door until Jen opened it. Gracie bounded from the back deck to the yard in one leap and ran around the corner to the front of the house. She ran to the end of the driveway where she sat in rapt attention, awaiting the first glimpse of her friend.

Watching Gracie's anxious anticipation brought a sweet memory to the forefront of Jen's mind—one of her beloved granddad. She had adored each of her grandparents, but both were gone now. It still made Jen tear up when special memories of them came to mind. The bond she shared with her granddad had been especially strong.

As a little girl, Jen couldn't have imagined anyone stronger, smarter, or more talented than him. He could build anything, fix anything, and make anyone laugh—especially her. As a young girl, she once told him that he was stronger than Superman and nicer than Santa Claus. He was a simple and humble man who worked hard to earn a modest living for his family, but to his granddaughter he was more important than royalty.

I was just like you, Gracie, she thought with a smile. *Waiting at the front door for my best friend to pull into the driveway.*

Now Gracie was standing in the driveway, looking across the street. Darcy was with her human, just outside their front door. Gracie's back end started to wiggle. With raised ears, an outstretched tail, and a straight back, she was the picture of controlled energy.

But the moment Darcy's owner released her to cross the street and she stepped onto Gracie's driveway, the Golden's energy was released, and the dogs leapt toward each other with their version of a hug before engaging in a high-speed game of chase. They streaked across the yard, barking happily, then sporadically came to an abrupt halt to sniff the ground and then each other before repeating the cycle.

Jen laughed as she watched their antics. Yet the memory of her granddad still lingered in her mind. As Gracie ran circles of sheer joy around Darcy, Jen could almost feel her granddad wrap her in a bear hug.

"I love you, too," she whispered, wrapping her arms tightly around her middle.

A moment later Darcy's owner approached from one direction, and the two dogs ran toward Jen from the other direction, inviting her to romp with them. Granddad would have approved.

PAWS & PONDER...

Why is a good name better than riches? What kinds of attributes give someone a good name?

Who would you consider to be someone with a "good name"? What characteristics made you select that person? What do you hope people think about when they hear your name?

_____  _____

Paws & Pray

Lord, help me to pursue a good name over fame and riches. Let me be known for my integrity, love, humility, and kindness. Lord, your name is the greatest name of all. Thank you for being an example I can emulate.

We may make our plans,
but God has the last word.

PROVERBS 16:1, GNT

LITTLE CESAR

We may make our plans,
but God has the last word.

PROVERBS 16:1, GNT

EMILY KNEW EXACTLY THE KIND of dog her family needed: a medium to large breed with a temperament calm enough to be a good companion for their aging dog, Sadie, but energetic enough to make a good playmate for her two young boys.

Encouraged to visit the local humane society facility where her friend Julie volunteered, Emily and her family went in search of their new dog.

The first canine they encountered was a small terrier mix that was barking incessantly in his crate. His bark set Emily's teeth on edge. The noise, his crazed look, and his small size eliminated him as a possibility in Emily's mind. She crossed him off the list and kept walking.

Next, they headed toward several rooms where rows of kennels and crates provided temporary housing for dogs in need of a permanent home. Emily's family members played with several large-breed dogs. But none was a good fit. Either the dogs needed a home without other animals, couldn't be trusted around children, or were too old. Emily really wanted a younger dog, one who would be there for her boys when Sadie was gone.

Emily felt discouraged. She had been certain they would find their new dog at the shelter.

As Emily's family prepared to leave, Julie brought out the terrier mix they had seen when they first arrived.

"His name is Cesar and he was found living on the streets. Would you like to spend some time with him before you go?"

I'm sorry you've had a hard life, Cesar, but you're not right for our family, Emily thought.

As she opened her mouth to say no, her older son said yes.

Cesar could be described in one word: wild. He ran in circles around Julie, almost knocking Emily's son over in the process. He barked, he jumped, and much to Emily's chagrin, the dog lifted his leg on her son's pant leg.

Yet as wild as he was, he was also playful, full of personality, and quite funny. He was like sunshine wrapped in fur. And although Emily kept reiterating their need for a larger dog, Julie suggested taking Cesar home for a trial stay. The shelter had recently implemented a program where prospective adoptive families could take a dog home on Friday and bring him back on Tuesday, in order to get a better idea of how the dog would fit into their family.

From the moment Cesar entered their home, he seemed to fit. He sat at Emily's feet as she prepared dinner. He followed Sadie around, even getting her to play a little bit with him. And he made the boys giggle continually with his antics. They had only known life with a senior dog, but Cesar played with the boys until they all collapsed from exhaustion.

When Tuesday came, the boys begged Emily to let them keep Cesar—even offering to pay the adoption fee from their Christmas and birthday money. But Emily still had doubts. After all, Cesar could not have been more different from the picture she had in her mind of their next dog.

And yet, something about Cesar's large brown eyes and fun-loving personality had won her heart.

"Yes, we can keep him."

Several months later, when they lost Sadie, Cesar helped mend their broken hearts. The little dog seemed to sense what each person in the family needed—sleeping with the boys, snuggling with Emily on the sofa, sitting quietly with her husband as he worked. Cesar was always there. Always ready to love and protect his family.

He might not have been the dog Emily would have chosen, but clearly God knew he was the exact dog her family needed.

Have you ever been convinced of something only to discover God had something totally different in mind for you? How did your feelings change throughout that process? Did you joyfully submit right away to his will? Or did it take awhile for you to accept it? Have you accepted it? Why is knowing who God is vital in being able to accept his will and plans for your life?

_____   🐾   _____

Paws & Pray

Lord, knowing who you are—your goodness and mercy, your righteousness and love—helps me to accept your will, especially when it is different from my own. And yet, even when I know you well, I can still struggle with accepting your will. Father, help me to trust you today more than I trusted you yesterday. Help me to trust that your plans are good, even when they don't feel good or seem to fit me. Let me believe that you are for me and not against me.

GYPSY'S TREASURES

Keep my words and treasure up my commandments with you.

PROVERBS 7:1, ESV

NICOLE SAT BACK ON HER KNEES to survey her work. Twenty bright orange marigolds now lined the walkway to her front door. As she patted the soil around the cheerfully colored plants, the corner of a foil wrapper caught her eye. She took her spade and unearthed a protein bar still in its wrapper.

Who would bury a protein bar? she pondered as she threw it in the garbage can.

A few days later her son Landon walked in the back door carrying a plastic bag containing the remnants of a loaf of bread.

"Uh, Mom?" he asked. "Why did you bury the bread?"

Landon had discovered the bag, half covered with dirt in their patchy side yard, when he was mowing. He had also found an empty water bottle and some loose magazine pages.

Over the next few weeks, they discovered more and more buried items: plastic grocery bags, a banana peel, an old flip-flop, and a pair of gardening gloves—which Nicole hadn't seen in months.

Nicole's family had three dogs—two Yorkshire terriers and a chocolate Lab, Gypsy. Nicole immediately eliminated the Yorkies as suspects; they didn't even like the feel of grass on their paws. *Gypsy!*

And sure enough, the next day Nicole watched another caper unfold from start to finish. That afternoon she was throwing what was left of Landon's lunch into the trash, including an empty Gatorade bottle, when Gypsy ran through the doggie door. As she resumed other tasks, Nicole saw Gypsy sneak the bottle out of the garbage and run back outside.

She then watched from the kitchen window as Gypsy frantically dug a hole near the deck and dropped her treasure inside. After pawing the dirt back over the bottle, Gypsy lay down several feet in front of her concealed plunder.

"You silly dog," Nicole said and chuckled, completely baffled by her dog's pirate-like behavior.

Nicole and her family tried to break Gypsy of her burying habit, but the dog was determined to keep a secret stash of miscellaneous household items and trash. As Gypsy got older, she even began burying things inside the house—pushed under blankets, stashed in piles of dirty laundry, or shoved under the sofa.

Over time Nicole realized the things Gypsy buried were items Nicole's family had touched, eaten, or used. Treats, toys, trash. If her humans had touched it, Gypsy wanted to keep it.

"You keep some funny treasures, Gypsy," Nicole said one night, rubbing the now white fur on her dog's muzzle. "But you gotta keep what's important close to you, huh?"

Nicole cast a glance at the coffee table that held a family photo and her well-worn Bible—the Bible she had treasured and held close for decades.

"Me too, baby girl," she said, warmth spreading through her heart. "Me too."

PAWS & PONDER . . .

Why is it important for us to keep and treasure God's Word? By keeping his Word in our minds, we are able to treasure it in our hearts. What are some practical ways you can keep Scripture in your mind and in your heart this week? What is one verse you will commit to memory this month?

----- 🐾 -----

Paws & Pray

Father, thank you for the gift of your Word. When I read it, I believe you are personally speaking to me. Give me a passion and the desire to keep your words in my mind and in my heart. God, help me treasure your words above all others.

Don't lose sight of common sense and discernment.

Hang on to them.

PROVERBS 3:21

10

CHAMP

If you become wise, you will be the one to benefit.
If you scorn wisdom, you will be the one to suffer.

PROVERBS 9:12

BRIAN, TABATHA, AND THEIR THREE teenage sons, Josiah, Caleb, and Seth, loved vacationing at Tabatha's parents' hundred-acre farm in Georgia. But this year they weren't the only ones who would enjoy the rural getaway. Their dog, Champ, a pointer-setter mix, was anxiously awaiting his first visit.

When they arrived, Champ could hardly believe his eyes. Back home, he had supervised access to a two-acre backyard. Here, it seemed the property went on forever.

Champ took full advantage of his freedom, spending it in perpetual motion. There were children to play with, squirrels to chase, ponds to swim in, and ATVs to race. Champ was constantly on the go.

After breakfast on the second day, Brian sat on the front porch of the house with Tabatha, watching Champ run at full speed behind the boys on the ATVs. "I don't think he's stopped moving since we arrived," Brian observed.

And other than a few brief naps, the hunting dog hadn't. As if he were intoxicated by boundless freedom, Champ ran haphazardly through fields and wooded areas, swam laps in the pond, and was continually on alert for squirrels.

On day four, when Tabatha was getting Champ's dinner ready, she noticed he was limping. "Brian, something's wrong with Champ."

"Come here, boy," Brian said. "Let me take a look." Brian gently ran his hand down the leg Champ was favoring, then turned the dog's foot over.

44

"I see the problem." Brian quickly examined each of Champ's paws. "Some of his pads are completely raw."

"Poor thing," Tabatha empathized.

Champ's freedom—and lack of restraint—had come at a price.

Brian gave Champ a bath and confined him to his outdoor kennel that night. The next day, much to the dog's dismay, he was kept on a fifty-foot leash in the yard. In fact, this was how Champ spent the rest of his vacation. Day after day, his woeful eyes sought out a sympathetic human to take pity on him and let him run free again.

"Sorry, bud," Tabatha said when his pleading eyes found her. "You need to heal. Clearly, you need some self-control in your life."

Several months later, a healed and healthy Champ returned to the farm with his family. Hoping Champ had learned his lesson, Brian opened the car door. Champ scrambled out and took off. Wisely, Brian and Tabatha monitored his activity this time, stepping in when necessary and making Champ rest his paws.

To this day, Champ would choose to run the pads off each paw if given the opportunity. But he has a loving family who wants to keep him safe.

PAWS & PONDER...

In what ways can too much freedom be dangerous? Have you or someone you love ever suffered harmful consequences when you scorned wisdom?

Paws & Pray

Lord, you have made wisdom available to me—in your Word, in others' advice, and even in my own body—when I listen. And yet so often I am tempted to disregard wisdom and go my own way. Help me choose to pursue the insight you offer and be grateful when you lovingly restrain me.

11

PRAYING FOR PIPPA

Anxiety weighs down the heart,
but a kind word cheers it up.

PROVERBS 12:25, NIV

PATTI WAS ANXIOUS. *But probably not as anxious as Pippa will be when Terri and Joe leave*, she thought. Pippa, a Maltese mix, adored Patti's sister and brother-in-law. Whenever Joe traveled for work, Pippa would get so upset she would refuse to eat or go outside.

Now both of them were going on a mission trip. How would little Pippa react to both Joe *and* Terri leaving her for two weeks?

When Terri asked Patti if she could watch Pippa, she couldn't say no. Patti knew she needed to be there for the dog. And besides, Patti's son, Cal, loved Pippa and was looking forward to taking care of her.

So Patti agreed and began to pray for the dog.

Patti suspected that whenever Joe and Terri were gone, the little dog believed her dear ones were lost forever and she mourned that they would never return. Patti decided to ask God to turn the little dog's mourning into joyful dancing.

Patti was diligent in her prayers for Pippa and recruited Cal and her husband, Wendel, to pray too. Even before Terri and Joe left on their trip, Patti would go over and spend time with Pippa, assuring her about all the fun they would have together. Patti even spoke Bible verses over her.

"Psalm 30:11 says God can turn mourning into dancing, Pippa. So we trust him to cause your little heart to dance with joy even while Joe and Terri are gone."

Finally, the day of Terri and Joe's departure arrived—along with the real test of how Pippa would react.

Patti tried to walk in the house with great confidence when she went by to check on Pippa, claiming every promise she had prayed over the dog. And yet, the truth was, she was a little panicky.

Would God answer a prayer for a dog's mental health?

From the moment Cal opened the door, Pippa began jumping and whimpering in joy. She ran circles around Cal, Patti, and Wendel. Pippa grabbed her tennis ball and dropped it at Cal's feet, clearly wanting to play fetch.

After several minutes of play, Patti watched in awe as Pippa ran to her food and water bowl and looked at Patti as if to say, "I'm ready for dinner now." And when Pippa scampered out through her doggie door to take care of her business, Patti couldn't hold back a shout of delight.

Since that time, Pippa has never had any issues when Terri and Joe go abroad for mission trips, and Patti and her family are always overjoyed to take care of her.

Pippa's worry and sadness were no match for Patti's words of kindness and prayer. Nor were they any match for the God whose grace extends even to the animals his children love so much.

PAWS & PONDER...

What has you in knots today? Will you take some time to read the Bible and allow God's kind words to infuse your heart with joy? Can you remember a time when someone prayed for you and spoke kind words to you, and your burden was lightened? Will you pray and ask God to allow you to speak words of kindness and life to someone today?

Paws & Pray

Lord God, so often I am anxious about situations, big and small. I know that you ask me to bring all my cares to you. I believe you hear my requests; I have witnessed answers to prayer so many times. I bring everything to you, praising your name, my true source of joy and peace.

Gentle words are a tree of life.

PROVERBS 15:4

12

A JOB FOR PEPPER

Laziness leads to poverty;
hard work makes you rich.

PROVERBS 10:4, CEV

PEPPER LOVED TO WORK. From the moment the black and gray Australian shepherd awoke in the morning, she had one important mission—retrieve the paper. Pepper took her job very seriously.

So seriously, in fact, that some Sundays when the paper was too thick and heavy to fit in her mouth, Pepper would push it toward the house with her nose. Her owners, Kathy and Mike, were both amused and inspired by her persistence.

One Sunday, the newspaper had landed partly in some bushes near the driveway, making it impossible for Pepper to push it with her nose. She dug at the paper, frantically trying to grab it. When Kathy noticed Pepper's predicament, she went outside to help.

"That's okay, girl," Kathy said, collecting the newspaper. "I'll get it today."

Kathy turned to walk back to the house, but Pepper didn't move.

The dog sat at attention—head cocked to the side, ears up, eyes focused on the paper in Kathy's hands.

"Come on, Pepper," Kathy called. "Let's go inside."

But Pepper remained motionless, still staring at the paper.

Impressed by the commitment her dog had to her job, Kathy slid the paper from the plastic sleeve, pulled out the city/state news section, and handed it over.

Kathy chuckled as Pepper proudly carried her section of the paper into the house. Granted, large areas were illegible smudges because of Pepper's drool. But the Aussie was proud of herself. She had been trained for a job, and she took pleasure in completing that job every day.

All hard work brings a profit.

PROVERBS 14:23, NIV

With the delivery completed, Pepper devoured a bowl of kibble, spent some time in the backyard, and enjoyed a belly rub before falling asleep at Kathy's feet—likely dreaming of thinner papers tossed in open areas.

As Kathy read the paper, her gaze kept drifting to Pepper. She couldn't help but be convicted.

"God," Kathy prayed, "make me more like my dog—eager and happy to do the work you set before me. Give me the confidence and perseverance to complete each task. And if I can't, please send someone to help me."

Still sleeping, Pepper let out a series of muffled yips that sounded like chuckles.

"And yes, Lord," Kathy added with her own laugh, "if you send someone to help me, I promise I will still do my part and carry my own section."

PAWS & PONDER...

How do you feel about work? Do you think today's proverb is referring only to monetary riches as a reward for hard work? What other kinds of riches might this verse be addressing? Is there a task God has given you that you haven't started? What is holding you back? Would you make a commitment to him right now to complete that task as an act of worship and love?

Paws & Pray

Lord, some days I am discouraged at work. Please help me see that no matter what I do, it is work that you have given me to do. If I need assistance, let me set aside my pride and seek it. I want to approach each task as an act of love and worship. Show me how to find that balance between hard work and rest that you desire for my well-being.

PERMISSION TO GRIEVE

The words of the reckless pierce like swords,
but the tongue of the wise brings healing.

PROVERBS 12:18, NIV

JUDY KNEW HER MOM was finally free from pain. The moment Grace's heart had stopped beating on this earth, her spirit had soared into the arms of her Savior. Judy also knew that she would see her mother again one day. And yet the pain she felt as the hospice nurse said, "She's gone," made it hard for her to breathe.

Judy reached down and stroked her black Lab's blocky head. Ever the devoted companion, the nine-year-old dog, Samson, hadn't left her side all morning. He had rarely left her mother's bedroom the past few days.

The three of them had been living together since Judy's father had died several years earlier. Judy was the youngest of four children and Grace's only daughter. The two had always been close, but their bond had grown even stronger since becoming roommates.

Now Judy excused herself from her mother's bedroom, thankful for the hospice nurse's capabilities and care. Samson followed her to the family room.

As Judy awaited her brothers' arrival, she began thinking of all the things she would need to do—make phone calls, plan a funeral service, schedule appointments, pay the bills. She swallowed hard, trying to keep her emotions in check so she could function. Yet the weight of responsibility began pressing in. *I can't fall apart now. There is too much to do.*

Her brothers arrived just before the coroner. Each of Grace's sons went to the back bedroom to say goodbye to "Muz," as they had lovingly called her.

Samson remained by Judy's side, but then he began pacing and panting. Judy tried to calm him down with a head scratch as she started writing her list.

The hospice nurse placed her hand on Judy's shoulder. "We're all set now and about ready to leave."

The nurse looked at Samson, who was panting nervously. "I think it might help him understand and relax if he can see and smell Grace one last time—to say goodbye."

Judy was numb as she and Samson followed the nurse to the stretcher where her mother's body lay. Samson sniffed Grace and nuzzled her. When she didn't respond, he whined and then he lay down.

"He needs time to grieve too," the nurse said, petting him gently.

Her words were meant for Samson, yet they wrapped around Judy's heart, giving her permission to mourn as well. As the hospice team wheeled the gurney from the house, Judy didn't try to stop the flood of tears. Her mother was gone, and it hurt.

Working through her to-do list could wait. Being strong could wait. Helping others could wait.

For the first time all day, Samson lay on his bed with his eyes closed. He seemed as exhausted from the weight of loss as Judy was.

"Thank you for staying with me," Judy told Samson. "You've always known just what I need."

PAWS & PONDER ...

The nurse's words brought healing to Judy's heart. What are some healing words that someone has said to you? Who needs your wise words of healing today?

Paws & Pray

Lord, I know I can be reckless with my words at times. Help me think before I speak, and show me people I can offer hope and healing to. I want to let go of the hurtful comments that others have said to me. Direct me to words of healing in your Word.

Whoever is patient has great understanding.

PROVERBS 14:29, NIV

14

HAPPY'S GIRL

Whoever is patient has great understanding,
but one who is quick-tempered displays folly.

PROVERBS 14:29, NIV

MAKING FRIENDS WAS DIFFICULT for three-year-old Olivia, whose temporary hearing loss during a critical period of her development had left her unable to communicate like most of the other children her age.

Her mother, Jackie, wanted nothing more for her daughter than to experience the joys and giggles of a happy, normal childhood. And yet day after day Olivia seemed to pull further and further into her own silent world. Sadly, it was a world in which playdates with other children simply didn't exist.

But then Happy joined the family. The pit bull mix had a perpetual smile, and he became Olivia's closest friend—a very large, very patient, unlikely best friend who was always delighted to play with the little girl he adored.

Often judged solely on his size and the reputation of the breed he most resembled, Happy continually surprised people who took the time to get to know him. His blocky head and stocky body housed the sweetest personality Jackie had ever known in a pet. It was the perfect temperament for playing with a three-year-old.

Jackie continually marveled at how calm, gentle, and patient Happy was with Olivia. He seemed to naturally understand her limitations, and he adapted to her communication style. A push against his side meant she wanted him to lie down, and a push against his rear meant he was to sit. Olivia had a distinct way to call him and he eagerly responded.

And yet, the thing that warmed Jackie's heart most was watching them play. Olivia would make Happy sit, place a teacup in front of him, and proceed to have a tea party with him. Other times Olivia would give Happy the special command to lie down so she could give him a thorough checkup with her Fisher-Price doctor's kit. Her daughter never seemed to run out of ideas. Like the time she attached a laundry basket full of stuffed animals to Happy's collar with a scarf and giggled nonstop when he took her toys on a bouncy ride across the room.

Happy was the ideal playmate for Olivia. He provided the perfect balance of sensitivity, playfulness, and companionship she needed at that time of her life.

Eventually, Olivia's hearing was restored, thanks to ear tubes and medication to clear the fluid in her ears. She began making significant strides in her communication skills, giving her the ability to make friends.

And yet, Happy still remained her most trusted confidant and closest friend. He was the one who understood her when many others could not, and he played with her when many others would not.

His patience and gentleness created a childhood for Olivia that she will always remember with fondness and joy.

He was her Happy, and she was his girl.

PAWS & PONDER...

In what ways does understanding produce patience? What are some blessings you might miss if you are unwilling to be patient? What blessings did Olivia receive from Happy's patience with her? What are some blessings you have received when you were patient?

—————————————————   ❀   —————————————————

Paws & Pray

Lord, you are the all-knowing, all-understanding, and most patient God. Thank you for extending patience to me. Please help me be patient with others. And Lord, just as Happy restrained himself and allowed Olivia to lead, help me to show humility and understanding to others so that I might be a blessing and show them a glimpse of your love.

Whoever gives heed to instruction prospers,
and blessed is the one who trusts in the LORD.

15

CODY ON THE GO

Whoever gives heed to instruction prospers,
and blessed is the one who trusts in the Lord.

PROVERBS 16:20, NIV

MELISSA'S PHONE BUZZED in her pocket.

"Running ten minutes late," the text from her neighbor Tish read. "Sorry."

Melissa slipped the phone back into her pocket and looked at her silver Lab's expectant expression.

"Sorry, Cody," she said, adjusting the leash that had gotten stuck under his back leg, "Gizmo's running a little late for our walk."

Cody, anxious to get moving, pulled on the leash.

"Okay, boy, I hear ya," she said. "We can walk for a bit while we wait for them."

Normally, Melissa and Tish kept a quick walking pace in the morning in order to get their active dogs as tired as possible before leaving them for the day. However, as Melissa waited for her friend and neighbor of seven years, she allowed Cody to set the pace. Melissa held the leash loosely in her hand and simply followed where he led. Cody was clearly thrilled with his freedom and investigated everything in sight. He sniffed bushes; he wandered into a clearing overlooking the creek that ran under the road. He discovered a turtle and attempted to play with it—until the odd-looking beast with the long leathery neck poked its head out of its shell.

Cody yelped in terror.

Melissa chuckled as she pulled him to safety on the other side of the road.

Cody recovered quickly from his fright and resumed his leisurely walk-and-sniff. Melissa enjoyed watching him explore. She laughed at his escapades and smiled at his discoveries. She even snapped a picture of Cody creeping back toward the turtle near the creek. But when the turtle's head emerged from its shell again, Cody dashed back to the road.

"No, Cody!" Melissa shouted, tightening up on the leash and pulling him back just as a car went by.

After redirecting him to another open area, Melissa again relaxed her hold on the leash.

Once again free to explore, Cody sniffed dandelions and pawed at a rock. But as he headed for a mud puddle, Melissa gave a quick tug on his leash.

"No, Cody!" she commanded.

The dog looked at her, then strained against the leash, wanting desperately to get to the enticing mud. Knowing how much he hated baths, Melissa pulled him back.

"Trust me, Codes," she said, urging him back to her side. "You aren't gonna like where that mud leads."

She clicked her tongue and started dragging an insistent and disgruntled Cody back toward Gizmo's house. He barked his displeasure and he thrashed his head, trying to break free. Melissa was grateful for the new, more secure harness he now wore. Several weeks earlier he had wiggled out of the collar and chased a squirrel for half a block. Cody was lovable and playful, but he was also headstrong and opinionated.

"Come on, boy," Melissa panted. "Let's go find Gizmo."

Cody stopped mid-tug. The mud was immediately forgotten when Cody heard the name Gizmo, and he eagerly pulled Melissa toward his beagle friend's house.

As Melissa followed her spirited dog, she realized how much she was just like her dog. God gave her so much freedom. And surely he delighted in watching her experience every blessing he had given her. Yet how many times had she pulled against his plans for her? How much trouble could she have avoided if she had heeded his warning? And how many messes did she create by insisting on going her own way?

She drew Cody to her side, kneeling to hug him close.

Whispering a prayer of repentance and thanksgiving, Melissa planted a kiss on Cody's head.

A slobbery kiss across her face ended her prayer. As she stood, she caught a glimpse of Gizmo and Tish heading their way.

"I see Gizmo!" she told her panting Lab.

And with those words Cody was off—with Melissa sprinting right behind.

PAWS & PONDER...

We have great freedom in Christ, and yet, in his love, he has set boundaries for us—to protect us and spare us from unnecessary pain. How often do you try to push past divine boundaries, insisting you know better? What mud puddle are you heading toward today? What might happen if you insist on going your own way? Are you willing to trust God and walk back to him?

Paws & Pray

Lord, so often I think I know better than you. I strive to go my own way and pull away from you. Father, forgive me and draw me back to you. Help me to trust your plan more than my own. And give me courage to walk away from the mud puddles of this life and walk on clear paths with you.

The hope of the righteous brings joy.

PROVERBS 10:28, ESV

16

I GOTCHA

The hope of the righteous brings joy,
but the expectation of the wicked will perish.

PROVERBS 10:28, ESV

AFTER THREE YEARS OF APARTMENT LIFE, Cora and her husband, Dillon, were delighted to move into a three-bedroom house. The new location meant a shorter commute for Dillon; miles of tree-lined sidewalks for walking their black and white cocker spaniel, Max; and friendly neighbors. The neighborhood was idyllic—with one cantankerous exception. A sandy-colored terrier mix seemed offended by this new dog on the block. He would stick his nose through the fence surrounding his yard, baring his teeth and barking ferociously whenever Cora and Max walked by. Max, a sweet-natured and timid dog, would scurry past the terrier's house, keeping Cora between himself and the cranky canine.

For an entire week the terrier sounded his disapproval, but with the fence as a barrier, Cora wasn't too concerned.

However, one morning when Cora and Max set out, they were startled to see the terrier racing down the sidewalk toward them, viciously barking. Instinctively, Cora scooped up Max into her arms, raised her leg to block the aggressor, and with a power she didn't know she possessed, she shouted, "No! Enough!"

The dog not only stopped—he sat.

A moment later a woman came running up with a leash.

"Is everyone okay? I'm so sorry this happened. I'm watching Scout while my friend is out of town. I didn't realize he snuck out my front door when I went to get the newspaper."

As the frazzled dogsitter took charge of Scout, she continued to apologize. "Are you sure no one was hurt? I promise to keep a closer eye on Scout."

"Thank you. Max and I are fine," Cora assured her. "Ready to go, Max?" Cora put him down on the sidewalk and they began walking. Having come through his ordeal unscathed, Max seemed to walk with his tail held a little higher and with an extra little bounce in his step.

He glanced at Cora. The look of adoration and gratitude warmed her heart.

"I gotcha, buddy. I'll always have your back," she said.

The rest of the walk was pleasantly peaceful.

The next morning Cora braced herself for another showdown with Scout. But it never happened. In fact, the little dog never barked at them again. He simply watched with interest as Cora and Max walked by. "You're actually kind of a cute little curmudgeon," Cora admitted.

When Scout finally went home to his owner, Cora missed seeing the testy dog when she and Max went on their walks. But one look at a much happier Max confirmed he liked everything just the way it was.

PAWS & PONDER...

Max placed his hope in Cora to protect him. In what ways did Max's hope lead to joy? In what or whom are you placing your hope? Is the source of your hope giving you joy?

Paws & Pray

Lord, you alone are my hope and the source of true joy. Right now, I place my hope and trust in you and ask that you would fill me with deep and abiding joy.

17

CONVINCING RAVEN

I am teaching you today—yes, you—
so you will trust in the Lᴏʀᴅ.

PROVERBS 22:19

RAVEN HAD NO IDEA she could swim. The black flat-coated retriever had no idea she had come from a long line of swimmers and champion dock divers. Or how dog-paddling was woven into her DNA. All she knew was leg-shaking, tail-tucking fear when she stood in front of a body of water.

And yet, her family knew she could swim. They knew about her bloodlines and her breed's natural love of the water. And they believed in her ability, even though she had not yet discovered it.

Each time Raven's family took her to the state park near their home, they hiked up to the lake, hoping this would be the time she would overcome her fear.

They had tried everything over the two years since they'd brought her home. They would toss sticks in the water, which she would gladly chase after—until the water got to her chest, at which point she would hightail it back to the shore. Anne had purchased a life vest for Raven, thinking that would make a difference.

It didn't.

On this outing, Anne's husband, Daniel, had carried Raven into the lake, vowing to hold her and let her get used to the feel of the water.

She clawed her way out of his arms, used his head as a springboard, and jumped back to shore.

Their children, fourteen-year-old Jackson and eleven-year-old Rachel, had even gotten in the lake and demonstrated the doggie paddle for Raven.

But Raven wanted no part of this experiment.

"Maybe it's just not worth it," Daniel mumbled the following evening. "So Raven doesn't swim. Is that really such a big deal?"

Anne wanted to agree with him. Raven didn't need to know how to swim. It wasn't like they lived on a houseboat and she needed to learn to swim in case she accidentally fell overboard. There were many other things Raven loved—taking walks, playing ball, catching Frisbees.

But they had seen how much their other dogs had loved swimming and knew what good exercise it was. Anne wanted to convince Raven of her own ability and, more important, to teach her that she could overcome her fear.

Anne knew firsthand how much fear could cost someone.

How many places had her intense fear of flying kept her from visiting? How many sleepless nights had her fear of something bad happening to her children cost her? And how many opportunities had she lost to her fear of failure?

Anne wanted more for her dog. And for herself.

The next weekend, Anne's family once again took Raven to the lake. But this time, they brought a different helper—Raven's best canine friend, Lady, an avid swimmer.

The moment Lady saw the water, she bounded in. Raven, caught up in chasing her friend, followed Lady into the lake but quickly put on the brakes once the water got deeper. Lady glanced at Raven as if to say, "C'mon. What are you waiting for?"

Lady swam over to Raven, whose feet were rooted to the rocky bottom.

Lady barked. Then play-bowed. And then leapt around, splashing and swimming back and forth in front of Raven.

Raven looked at the shore.

"You can do it, girl. Just try," Anne whispered from the shore, not knowing whether she was encouraging her dog or herself.

Raven looked back at Lady.

Anne could see the longing in her dog's eyes. The familiar look of yearning warring with fear.

Anne held her breath as Raven's front legs began to move.

She grabbed her husband's arm as the retriever's back legs left the rocky bottom.

And she whooped and hollered as her dog began the most hilarious dog paddle she had ever seen.

With her front legs completely straight, she kicked them up and down in what looked like a high-stepping march.

But the more time Raven spent in the water with her friend, the more relaxed she (and her swimming style) became. In less than twenty minutes, the dog who had been terrified of the water was swimming side by side with her best buddy.

"You did it!" Anne praised Raven when the dogs emerged from the lake.

Anne hugged Raven close and then hugged Lady, two dripping-wet friends.

"Thank you for being out there with my girl," she told Lady. "She trusted you, and you didn't let her down."

As Anne stood up, she looked heavenward and made a commitment to God. "I'm willing to try, too, because I know I can trust you."

PAWS & PONDER...

What fear has you shaking on the shore? What is it you are afraid will happen if you step into the water? Take a moment to write down your fear. Next to that fear write down everything you know to be true of God. God is bigger than any fear you will ever have. And he is right there with you. Remind yourself you can trust God. He is holding you, even now. And he will never let you go.

Paws & Pray

Lord, fear distorts my vision. Fear causes me to see it as bigger than you. God, lift my eyes toward you today. Lift my head up and allow me to see things clearly. Allow me to see you as greater than anything. Enable me to take the first steps of faith toward you. I trust you, Father.

As water reflects the face,

so one's life reflects the heart.

PROVERBS 27:19, NIV

18

WHAT DID YOU DO?

The greedy stir up conflict,
but those who trust in the Lord will prosper.

PROVERBS 28:25, NIV

BILLY COULDN'T WAIT for his grandparents to meet his newest dog, a reddish-brown hound mix he had named Red. Billy had seen the stray from time to time in their 1950s rural Kentucky neighborhood. But once Red wandered into nine-year-old Billy's yard, the hound dog had stayed close to his adopted home and his adopted boy.

On the day the family was getting ready to visit Billy's grandparents who lived an hour away, Billy's dad said, "Red's not coming."

Billy couldn't believe what he'd just heard.

"But Red's gonna be so lonely all by himself."

"He managed just fine before finding you," Billy's dad reminded his son.

"Mama?" Billy whined, turning the full force of his pleading blue eyes on his softhearted mother. "You would never leave one of your kids behind, right? Red is my responsibility, and I need to take care of him."

Billy squeezed out some tears to seal the deal, and his parents relented. Red could join the family on their overnight visit.

When they arrived, Red bounded out of the car and headed toward the creek. Billy started to chase after the dog, but his dad pulled him back.

"First, you say hello to your grandparents. That dog can fend for himself for a bit," he said.

Billy greeted his grandparents with a hug and politely listened to the grown-ups discuss boring things like crops, relatives' illnesses, and taxes. After a while, Billy asked to be excused.

He snuck a piece of bread from the kitchen on his way out.

"Red! Come here, boy," he yelled. "Where are ya?"

A moment later Billy heard a ruckus coming from a neighboring farm—chickens were squawking and screaming. Then he heard the neighbor, Mr. Groon, shouting. Just as Billy started back to the house, Red sprinted toward him—yellow ooze dripping from his mouth.

"There you are!" Billy said, intercepting his dog. "Whatcha been doin'? And what's on your face?"

Just then, the back door of his grandparents' house slammed.

"Billy!" his dad bellowed.

"Uh-oh. You'd better stay here," Billy told Red.

Red dropped to the ground in a perfect down-stay and didn't move a muscle.

"That dog of yours broke into Mr. Groon's chicken coop and grabbed about a dozen eggs," Billy's dad said. "You need to keep that dog outta there, you hear?"

"Yes, sir," Billy replied.

That night Billy gave his dog an extra bowl of kibble and a piece of pecan pie, hoping to dissuade him from another egg heist.

But Red had tasted the forbidden yolk and wanted more.

Later that night Billy was awakened to a cacophony of sounds: terrified chickens, barking dogs, shouting people, and a braying donkey.

Suddenly, Red was at the back door, the evidence of his guilt all over his jowls.

Billy's heart raced when he heard Mr. Groon's voice boom, "I've got a shotgun, and I'm not afraid to use it!"

Billy looked sheepishly at his parents who had woken up and stumbled out of the guest room. Granddad handed Billy a long rope, and he went outside to secure his thieving dog to a nearby tree. Billy was relieved they were leaving in the morning.

Billy knew the hound couldn't be trusted to behave at his grandparents', so he never asked if Red could come with them again. He just made sure Red was cared for when they went.

It turns out Billy's dad was right. Red did just fine without Billy for a couple of days. But he was always glad when Billy came home.

PAWS & PONDER...

In what ways can greed stir up conflict? What kinds of conflict have you experienced because you were greedy? In what ways does trusting the Lord help us prosper? Do you think this refers only to monetary prosperity? How have you prospered by trusting the Lord?

_____  _____

Paws & Pray

Lord, you are my greatest reward. Help me to trust you more each day. Forgive me for the times I'm greedy and not content with what I have. Enable me to see and value the gifts and blessings you have given me, and stir my heart to want to share those with others.

Listen to my instruction and be wise. Don't ignore it.

PROVERBS 8:33

19

RING THE BELL

Listen to my instruction and be wise. Don't ignore it.

PROVERBS 8:33

CALLIE WAS ECSTATIC. Finally, after twenty-eight long years of waiting, she had her very own puppy—a brown Lab mix named Hershey. She picked up the nine-week-old puppy and snuggled him next to her face.

"I've waited so long for you, little one," she whispered. Before this moment, she had never felt her life was settled enough for such a responsibility, but now she felt fully prepared.

After finalizing the paperwork with the shelter, Callie secured Hershey in her car and took him home.

As soon as Hershey was old enough, Callie enrolled him in puppy school.

One evening, the instructor explained bell training—a method of potty training your dog by hanging a bell from the door knob and teaching the dog to ring the bell as a signal to go outside.

Callie was intrigued with the idea. She went home that night and hung a bell from a ribbon and attached it to the doorknob. At first Hershey was far more interested in playing with the bell. But Callie would ring it every time she opened the door to take him out. After a few days, she began using a treat to lure Hershey's nose to the bell, having him nudge it before opening the door.

Several weeks later, Callie was in the kitchen and heard a merry tingling sound. Hershey was standing by the door, nosing the bell to go out. "You are a genius, Hershey! Let me get your leash."

Hershey was rewarded with a trip outside and a handful of kibble treats.

From that day on, Hershey always rang his bell when he needed to go outside, and Callie always responded quickly to let him out.

When Hershey was two years old, Callie was upstairs working from home on a blustery day when she heard him ring his bell. She quickly got up and walked to the door, only to find Hershey with her slipper in his mouth.

"What are you doing, boy?" she asked, chuckling.

She opened the door, but Hershey didn't move.

Callie took a step toward her dog when suddenly he turned and ran into the family room, Callie in pursuit.

"Hershey, what has gotten into you?" she said, removing her slipper from his mouth.

Callie went back upstairs.

A few minutes later, Hershey rang the bell again. This time when Callie got to the stair landing, she saw Hershey standing at the bottom of the stairs with a water bottle in his mouth.

"Hershey!" she scolded. "Drop it."

When she took the first step down, Hershey took it as his cue to bolt. Hershey sprinted through the house, with Callie on his heels.

Three times around the sofa they went, and Callie had to stop.

She collapsed on the sofa and laughed.

"You little stinker! I guess you decided to train me on the bell too, huh? *Ring the bell and make Mommy chase me!* You really are a smart and silly dog."

Hershey thumped his tail in agreement.

PAWS & PONDER...

How does listening to God's instruction make a person wise? Have you been ignoring an instruction from the Lord? What is keeping you from obeying? Are you willing to take a step of obedience today?

---　✿　---

Paws & Pray

Father, you are so wise. Forgive me for the times I choose not to listen to you. I love you and want to obey you. Keep giving me examples that I can learn from. Open my eyes and help me realize these are ways you show how much you care.

ELSA WON'T LET GO

Joyful are those who listen to me,
watching for me daily at my gates,
waiting for me outside my home!

PROVERBS 8:34

THE FIRST TIME ASHLEY DROVE HOME from the grocery store and found her Akita, Elsa, sitting in the front yard, she didn't think much of it. She had left the two-year-old dog inside the house, but Ashley assumed her husband had let the dog out just before she got home. When Ashley opened the car door, Elsa leapt onto her lap. Her happy cries and sounds made Ashley laugh.

The next time Ashley drove up to find Elsa sitting by the driveway, she asked her husband how long their dog had been outside. "She started whining as soon as you left so I let her outside." Then, looking a bit sheepish, he added, "I forgot she was there."

The third time Ashley pulled up to find Elsa sitting at attention at the top of the driveway, she suspected her dog was actually waiting for her.

Ashley shouldn't have been surprised—after all, Elsa waited for her outside the bathroom door, lay at her feet when she was working on her computer or at her desk, and slept on the floor next to her side of the bed at night. But Elsa's front-yard vigil deeply touched Ashley's heart.

Something about her dog choosing to wait outside for her, ignoring all the distractions on their street, and then racing to greet her the minute she got out of her vehicle made Ashley choke up.

Elsa was the picture of loyalty and devotion.

Over the next few months, whenever Ashley left and someone else was home,

Elsa would whine at the back door until she was allowed outside to sit vigil for Ashley's return.

It got to the point that Elsa could identify Ashley's car from six houses away.

Her eyes were always searching for it, her ears listening for the voice of the human she adored.

Elsa became Ashley's living, breathing, tail-wagging picture of what it looks like to wait in anticipation and joy for God—waiting for him to answer a prayer, waiting for him to reveal his plan, watching for evidences of his grace. The loyal dog also served as a beautiful picture of the delight God surely feels when his beloved children come home to him.

PAWS & PONDER . . .

Are you waiting on God for something? Are you watching with joyful anticipation? Or does your wait feel more like a burden? What evidences of God's grace have you seen recently—either in your life or someone else's?

Paws & Pray

Father, thank you for loving me. Thank you for delighting in each one of your children and rejoicing when a person comes to faith through your Son. God, because you love me, I know I can trust you—even when the waiting is long. Fill my heart with joy and anticipation as I wait and hope in you.

A longing fulfilled is sweet to the soul.

21

SUNNY'S HEDGEHOG

A peaceful heart leads to a healthy body;
jealousy is like cancer in the bones.

PROVERBS 14:30

SUNNY HAD BEEN THE BABY of the family for four years. Darrell and Jen had adopted the reddish-blonde Golden retriever on their one-year anniversary, and since that time Sunny had enjoyed her only-child status. She accompanied them on road trips, was allowed on the furniture, and even was included in the family portrait.

Sunny reveled in the attention and was often teased by Jen and Darrell's friends and family for being a bit of a princess.

However, her diva-like status was about to take a major hit.

The first clue was when Darrell and Jen left for several days without her. This had never happened before. Sunny liked her pet sitter well enough, but she wanted her people back.

On a cold January morning, Darrell and Jen came home. When the front door opened, Sunny greeted Darrell with a welcome-home jump.

But before Sunny could greet Jen with an equally joyful jump, Darrell pulled her back by the collar and held her.

"Gentle, girl," he commanded.

Sunny's nostrils began to quiver, and she raised her nose to take in a new scent. She looked as though she were asking, *What is that? What is Jen carrying?*

Then a strange cry filled the room.

Jen sat down on the sofa, holding a squirmy bundle in her arms. She nodded at Darrell.

Darrell got a firmer grip on Sunny's collar and led the dog to the sofa.

Sunny wanted to jump up, but Darrell kept her in check. She sat in front of Jen and watched as Jen pulled the blanket back, revealing the tiniest human Sunny had ever seen.

Desperate to smell this newcomer, Sunny inched closer and closer. When she tried to lick the fidgety baby, Darrell pulled her back.

All day Sunny stayed close to Jen and the little person they called Andrew.

The next day, Sunny anxiously awaited her morning walk. But it never came. Darrell and Jen seemed more tired than usual. Sunny suspected the tiny human had something to do with their exhaustion.

Two days later, Sunny stood by the back door hoping to go for a ride in the car.

But Darrell and Jen never left the house. Instead, Jen's parents brought over some tasty-looking things called diapers. Sunny didn't know what they were, but she made it her mission to try to grab as many as she could—some tasted better than others.

Day after day, Sunny waited for her life to get back to normal.

But each day Jen and Darrell seemed busy with the baby. Holding him, feeding him, washing him, and talking to him.

Even though she was doing more observing than interacting, Sunny liked the little person. She felt a strong desire to guard and protect him, but she also missed being the focus of Darrell and Jen's attention.

Days passed. Sunny decided to take a different approach.

Jen was sitting on the sofa holding the baby, so Sunny walked over to her toy bin and picked up her large stuffed hedgehog. It wasn't quite as big as the baby, but it was close. She took her hedgehog over to the sofa and lay down with it nestled between her front paws.

Later, when Jen went into the nursery to feed the baby, Sunny lay down at Jen's feet and positioned her hedgehog against her belly.

And that night, when Darrell and Jen put the baby in a large dish inside of the big scary bathtub and began to wash him, Sunny dropped her hedgehog into the bathtub for a bath too.

For two whole weeks, everything Jen did with the baby Sunny mimicked with her hedgehog.

Darrell and Jen laughed and smiled a lot at Sunny—although Sunny didn't know why.

Then about a month after the baby's arrival, Darrell asked Sunny if she wanted to go for a ride. Sunny jumped out of her bed and ran to the door—leaving her hedgehog behind.

After that day, Sunny didn't play as much with her hedgehog. She didn't seem to need it anymore.

Her life wasn't like it was before, but it was okay. Now she had three family members to love.

Sunny suspected that by the way the baby was growing, someday he might be big enough to play with her. She was certain Andrew would be even more fun than her hedgehog.

PAWS & PONDER...

In what areas do you struggle most with jealousy? Do you long for peace and contentment in those areas? What are some differences between a peace-filled heart and a heart full of jealousy?

Paws & Pray

Lord, let me be someone who is marked by peace and contentment. Forgive me for being consumed by jealousy and envy. Father, I confess those feelings to you now and ask you to replace them with gratitude for what you've given me. Help me to embrace your perfect will for my life and release my insecurities to you.

The generous will prosper;

those who refresh others will themselves be refreshed.

PROVERBS 11:25

22

A MAJOR MINOR
CATASTROPHE

When the storms of life come, the wicked are whirled away,
but the godly have a lasting foundation.

PROVERBS 10:25

WHEN PAUL AND MARIANNE were given the shepherd mix by one of Marianne's former students, the couple thought long and hard about what to name him. He was highly intelligent with good instincts. He could find anything they hid in the yard and quickly learned the commands they taught him.

"He's so smart, he could be in the military," Paul said. "I bet he'd be a major."

And yet, as endearing as he was, he didn't have any concept of his size or strength within the confines of the house. He constantly plowed into Paul and Marianne, banged into furniture, and was always knocking things off shelves with his tail.

"He is a lovable catastrophe," Marianne joked.

Major Catastrophe.

Outdoors, Major had room to run, play with Paul and Marianne, and explore every inch of his fenced-in yard. They bought him a large insulated dog condo to sleep in, and he enjoyed being an outside dog . . . except when a storm was rolling in. Major was terrified of thunder and lightning, so the couple made sure he was in the house when the weather turned menacing.

One day as dark clouds began to fill the sky, Marianne opened the door to find Major standing there, looking concerned.

"C'mon, boy," she said, giving him a good scratch. "You're safe in here. Just try not to go berserk."

Just then, a bolt of lightning flashed and seemed to electrify the family room. Major shot across the room to Paul.

"You're fine," Paul reiterated to his dog. "Nothing is going to hurt you in here."

After several minutes, Major calmed down. He kept an ear tuned to the storm but began investigating the split-level house, going from room to room. He sniffed the bathroom and every inch of the downstairs family room before heading upstairs to the kitchen.

Suddenly, Major raced back down the stairs. Barking and whining, he stood in front of Marianne and Paul, blocking their view of the television.

"Shhh, Major. It's okay. The storm will be over soon," Marianne said.

Major ran over and pawed her arm, but she ignored him.

The dog raced up the stairs, then back down.

"Why are you in such a tizzy?" Marianne said, trying to grab his collar.

Major jumped back, barking and frantically circling around at the bottom of the stairs.

"Okay, I'm up," Marianne said, passing the remote to Paul. "What is the problem? Is there thunder upstairs?"

As soon as Marianne got to the top of the stairs, she stepped into a puddle of water! A pipe had burst under the sink and water was gushing everywhere.

"Paul!" she yelled. "Turn off the water to the house!"

Between the sound of the TV and the heavy rain outside, Marianne and Paul had not heard the flooding water upstairs.

Marianne hugged Major, thinking how much more damage they would have sustained if he hadn't alerted them.

They still had quite a mess to clean up, but thanks to Major, it was only a minor catastrophe.

PAWS & PONDER...

What are some catastrophes—major or minor—that you have faced? How did you get through them? In what ways is God a "lasting foundation"? If you are facing storms today, talk to the Lord about them.

Paws & Pray

Lord, you are my rock and my refuge, my secure and lasting foundation. Help me not to fear the storms of life but to trust you to hold me fast when they swirl around me. Be my safe place, my rescuer and my defender, Lord.

The wise store up knowledge,

but the mouth of a fool invites ruin.

PROVERBS 10:14, NIV

OH, CAPONE!

The wise store up knowledge,
but the mouth of a fool invites ruin.

PROVERBS 10:14, NIV

"OH, CAPONE!" is a phrase often heard in Babette's house.

With an appetite inversely proportional to his size, her eighteen-pound Miniature Pinscher has spent most of his days looking for food. He has tried to ingest anything he could get his mouth around—whether it was edible or not.

It started when Babette discovered her little chowhound trash-diving one evening. Babette began keeping the trash can in a cupboard—secured with a rubber band to the knob of the adjoining cupboard so Capone couldn't open it.

One night, after throwing out a rotisserie chicken carcass, a bolt of lightning lit up the sky, followed by a deafening clap of thunder that shook the house. Babette and her husband heard a loud cracking sound and then a huge crash.

"A tree's down!" They ran out the door to check on their neighbors. An eighty-foot oak had been hit by lightning and a gigantic branch had landed on the neighbors' house. No one was hurt, but there was damage to the chimney and roof.

A half hour later, Babette returned to a mess inside the house. The cupboard door was open and the trash can had been pulled out and was lying on its side. There was no sign of the chicken carcass in the trash strewn across the floor. In the corner of the kitchen was Capone with guilt written all over his face and a belly so swollen it appeared as though he were carrying a litter of twelve puppies!

"Oh, Capone," Babette lamented. "What have you done?"

She rushed him to the emergency vet, where X-rays confirmed that Capone had indeed ingested the entire chicken's skeletal remains. Somehow, he had gobbled everything whole. It was still intact inside his distended stomach! Babette stayed with Capone for hours in the exam room as the vet gave him medicine to try to expel the chicken.

The medicine eventually worked, and four X-rays later (at one hundred dollars per image) the vet finally declared Capone carcass-free. The entire ordeal cost twelve hundred dollars and left Capone with a permanent description in his file: Capone—the chicken carcass dog.

Babette hoped the chicken caper would teach Capone a lesson.

Months went by with no incidents. As summer was winding down, Babette and her husband decided to apply fresh caulk around the panes of their century-old farmhouse windows. Capone seemed interested in what they were doing, but their focus was on the windows, not him. Finally, the job was done, and it was time to clean up and take showers. About an hour later they walked downstairs and there was Capone—with white putty on his whiskers. The Min Pin had licked the caulk from each and every pane he could reach.

"Oh, Capone . . ." Babette gasped, frantic to find the tube of caulk.

When she found it, she didn't see any poison warning, but her instincts said, *Call the vet.*

After explaining the situation to the receptionist, Babette cringed when the woman said, "Oh, I remember Capone. He's the chicken carcass dog, right?"

"Yes," Babette said. "That's him."

The vet had never treated a dog that had eaten caulk before, but he decided the best course of action would be to induce vomiting with doses of hydrogen peroxide. Thankfully, it worked.

As it did months later when Capone raided the kids' Easter baskets and scarfed down all the Hershey kisses. And again when he ate a bar of Dial soap.

Oh, Capone . . .

PAWS & PONDER . . .

You probably don't ever plan to eat a whole chicken carcass (bones and all) or a tube of caulk, and yet "ruin" could still be invited in and out of your mouth. How often have you eaten something you knew wasn't healthy for you? Or said something unkind without even thinking? In what ways can wisdom protect you from such ruin? And how do you store that knowledge?

_____ 🐾 _____

Paws & Pray

God, you are the Author and Creator of wisdom. I often do and say things without even thinking of the consequences for myself or for others. Draw my heart and mind to you that I might speak with integrity and grace. Put your love in my heart and your words in my mouth.

A TALE OF TWO DOGS

Let love and faithfulness never leave you;
bind them around your neck, write them on the tablet of your heart.
Then you will win favor and a good name in the sight of God and man.

PROVERBS 3:3-4, NIV

ONE LOYAL DOG. One former president. One heartwarming photo on the internet—and suddenly the entire country knew the name Sully, the service dog to late President George H. W. Bush. The image of the yellow Labrador retriever lying dutifully in front of his flag-draped coffin became the embodiment of loyalty and honor to a grieving nation.

The two-and-a-half-year-old service dog had done his job well. He had provided companionship, acts of service, and loyalty to the former president in his final months. Even after the president's death, Sully remained in his service and at his side. Loyalty and faithfulness—traits that can leave a lasting impression on others, even if no one captures a viral-worthy photo or the world is unaware of an animal's name or story.

Such was the case with Samson—a black Lab belonging to a woman named Judy.

While Samson may share a name with a rather infamous Bible hero, the world never had reason to know this dog's name.

Samson never served a president nor aided a war veteran. And his humble act of service was never reported on the nightly news.

But the way Samson demonstrated loyalty and faithfulness to Judy's family makes him a hero in her eyes.

The midnight-colored Lab adored Judy's elderly parents, D. L. and Grace, whom he stayed with during the day when Judy worked.

Judy's dad would play ball with Samson for hours—oftentimes throwing the ball from a chair because the dog's endurance outmatched his own. If Samson wasn't playing catch with D. L., he was following him around like a shadow.

But then one day, D. L. became too sick to get out of bed. Thankfully, his "shadow" didn't seem to mind. Instead, Samson just climbed up next to him. As Judy and her mom, along with the hospice nurses, tried to make D. L. comfortable, Samson remained by his side in the bed.

Loyal and faithful.

Samson was with D. L. until he drew his last breath.

Then after taking a final sniff of his favorite ball thrower, Samson turned his attention to Grace and Judy.

He lay with Judy at night as she cried.

He sat with Grace each day as she mourned.

Samson's constant presence steadied both of them through the storm of grief and loss. The black Lab helped them find their way to a new normal.

He reminded them of sweet memories but also helped them build new ones.

Sully and Samson.

Two loyal dogs.

Two faithful companions.

Two very good names.

PAWS & PONDER...

Why are love and faithfulness so important in this world? Who would you consider a loyal and faithful person in your life? What do you want people to think about you when they hear your name?

⎯⎯⎯⎯⎯⎯⎯⎯⎯⎯⎯⎯⎯⎯⎯⎯ ❀ ⎯⎯⎯⎯⎯⎯⎯⎯⎯⎯⎯⎯⎯⎯⎯⎯

Paws & Pray

Lord, you tell me in your Word that you will never leave me nor forsake me. Thank you for being the perfect example of love and faithfulness. Help me honor your name by following your lead and living my life in the same way.

The light of the righteous shines brightly.

GOOD GIRL, GIDGET!

Direct your children onto the right path,
and when they are older, they will not leave it.

PROVERBS 22:6

GIDGET, A THREE-YEAR-OLD Goldendoodle, stood defiantly in the kitchen, trying to conceal the balled-up sock in her mouth. She eyed Kate, willfully disobeying the command she had just been given.

"Gidget, come," Kate repeated.

Her dog turned and took a step in the opposite direction.

Gidget was the most strong-willed dog Kate had ever known. She also happened to be the smartest dog she had ever known—traits Kate was becoming convinced might be related.

Kate had enrolled Gidget in puppy obedience school and learned that the Goldendoodle definitely had a strong will, but she also had a strong desire for treats.

Whenever Gidget obeyed Kate's commands, she received a treat, followed by the words, "Good girl, Gidget!"

Gidget had grown into a wonderful dog who brought joy into Kate's life. And yet, Gidget's willfulness remained fully intact. Kate couldn't break her from stealing socks.

Whenever Gidget snatched a sock, the commands she knew quite well, such as "drop it" and "come," were ignored.

However, recently Kate had made a fascinating discovery.

After a quick snatch-and-grab during laundry day, Kate had called for Gidget to come. As usual, the Goldendoodle feigned hearing loss. When Kate repeated the command, her elbow bumped into Gidget's bag of treats. The sound miraculously restored her dog's hearing, and Gidget took a step toward Kate. "Good girl, Gidget!" Kate said, encouraging her to come closer.

The moment the dog heard the words—maybe enhanced with the sound of possible treats—she ran to Kate.

Kate took the sock from Gidget's mouth, told her again what a good girl she was, and then tossed her a treat.

From that point forward, whenever Gidget chose to ignore a command, Kate would say "Good girl, Gidget!" and nine times out of ten the dog would obey.

In her early training, Gidget had made a connection between the words and the reward—and it had stayed with her all these years.

As Gidget stood in the kitchen with a defiant look in her eyes and a sock in her mouth, Kate simply smiled and said, "Good girl, Gidget! Come."

And she did.

Gidget walked to Kate, gave up the sock, and received a treat and a thorough bonus back scratch.

As Kate continued to praise her dog, she couldn't help but think about the benefits of early training. She was also reminded of the importance of being who you are—and believing what the one who really loves you believes about you.

PAWS & PONDER...

Today's proverb talks about directing your children toward the right path. What are some practical ways you direct your child toward the right path? Proverbs 22:6 is a principle, not a promise. What's the difference between the two? Have you done everything you can to "train up your child in the way he or she should go" only to watch them go toward the opposite path? Spend some time talking to God about that. Pray for that child today. And then ask God to help you surrender your child's faith journey to him, remembering God loves your child even more than you do!

Paws & Pray

O Father, it is so hard to watch children go their own way. I realize you know those feelings better than anyone. For those children who are struggling—who are choosing paths their family would have never chosen for them—please lead them back to you, in your perfect timing and will. And Lord, for those little ones being shown the path of life today, cement that path in their little hearts and illuminate it in their sweet souls so that its light may never dim and they may daily walk with you.

26

UNDERSTANDING LOLA

A person's thoughts are like water in a deep well,
but someone with insight can draw them out.

PROVERBS 20:5, GNT

FRUSTRATION SURGED THROUGH Bruce as he stared at his dog, Lola. The two-year-old border collie had been standing in the family room barking incessantly for the past five minutes.

"What?" Bruce bellowed, unable to take the sound anymore. "I took you outside. I fed you dinner. You've had a treat. What else could you possibly want?"

Lola stopped momentarily as she listened to Bruce's tirade, then resumed the cacophony.

Bruce's head was pounding. All he wanted to do was lie on the sofa and watch TV. His wife and kids were at a birthday party, and he was looking forward to a quiet evening—until Lola went berserk.

With his TV program on pause, Bruce got on the floor next to Lola and looked around, trying to see from her vantage point.

"Okay, girl, I see no bad guys. I smell no smoke. So, what is your deal?"

Lola flattened her body to the floor, turning her head toward the sofa. Bruce mimicked Lola's actions. And there, under the sofa, was Lola's favorite ball.

"Well, I'll be . . ." Bruce said, retrieving the ball for his dog. "Why didn't you just say your ball was stuck?" He laughed as he tossed the ball to Lola.

With her ball tucked safely in her mouth, Lola lay down on her bed, and Bruce finished watching the program.

Several days later Bruce and Lola were alone again when she started her rhythmic barking—this time while standing by the kitchen island. Bruce spotted the ball under the table. He tossed it to her. Lola didn't even try to catch it. She simply kept barking.

Here we go again, he thought, trying to figure out why Lola seemed distressed.

What are the symptoms of mad cow disease? Can dogs get it? Bruce tried to ignore Lola and clean off the island counter before heading into work.

As he lifted a discarded dish towel, he discovered someone's breakfast plate. There on the plate was half a banana, which happened to be Lola's favorite fruit.

Bruce looked at his dog, who had suddenly gone quiet. Her gaze was fixed on the banana in his hand. Two ribbons of drool streamed from her mouth.

"What?" Bruce teased. "You want this ol' thing? This sweet, yummy banana?"

He pretended to take a bite before tossing it to Lola.

Over the next several weeks, Bruce learned how to tell the difference between Lola's vocalizations. At first he had been irritated by her barking, but after taking the time to try to understand her behavior, he realized her barks were a sign of her high intelligence. She was communicating with him. Whether letting him know the cat wanted to come in, or she needed help retrieving a toy, or asking for a chunk of ice or for an invitation to sit with him on the sofa, Lola knew what she wanted and wasn't shy about asking.

All she needed from Bruce was a willingness to listen.

PAWS & PONDER...

So often a person gets stuck in "surface" conversation. You hear someone's words—or see her actions—but you don't take the time to look past the exterior and try to understand what the other person is really trying to say. Why is it important to listen and pay attention to those around you? You might be surprised by what you learn.

Paws & Pray

Father, I'm guilty of not really seeing and hearing others. I desire to engage with others in a way that brings them life and hope. I need your help to be that caring individual.

WHAT A FRIEND

Love prospers when a fault is forgiven,
but dwelling on it separates close friends.

PROVERBS 17:9

"READY TO GO VISIT?" Sandee asked Tesla.

Her two-year-old Golden retriever looked intently at her. A wagging tail, raised ears, and open mouth indicated Tesla was definitely ready. In fact, the more time Sandee spent with her sweet-natured dog, the more she believed Tesla had actually been *born* ready to work as a therapy dog. Even as a young puppy, the sandy-colored Golden had been unusually calm and even-tempered, crucial traits for a therapy dog.

Especially one like Tesla, who worked with advanced-stage Alzheimer's patients.

Sandee led her dog into the multipurpose room, where a handful of residents were assembled. A couple sat together at a table, two women slumped down in their wheelchairs, and a man stood holding tightly to a walker. A few sets of eyes, bright with awareness, lit up as Tesla walked into the room.

She happily went to the outstretched hands beckoning her to come. If someone did not reach for her, Tesla would look at Sandee for guidance.

"Is it okay if my dog says hello to you?" Sandee would ask the resident. Rarely did anyone say no. And the moment they said yes, Tesla was at their side.

A bright-eyed woman at the table patted her knees and called, "Good doggie-doggie." Tesla responded immediately. The woman smiled wide as she stroked Tesla's long coat and giggled when Tesla gave her a paw to shake.

But then without any warning, the woman smacked Tesla on the nose and started screaming, "You're being so mean to me! You're a bad dog!"

Tesla cast a quick glance at Sandee—seeking instruction or reassurance. Quick to give both, Sandee knelt before her dog, rubbed her chest, told her she was a good girl, and then instructed her to stay by her side as the nursing staff gently led the weeping woman back to her room. Sandee offered a silent prayer for the woman, whose disease was clearly at an advanced stage.

Although Sandee was a little shaken, Tesla went right back to work, happily visiting every patient who beckoned her.

Week after week, Sandee and Tesla returned to the Alzheimer's care floor, and week after week, Sandee watched her dog lavish everyone with affection, attention, and companionship. The incident with the confused woman had not fazed Tesla at all. The dog held no grudge. And she wasn't the least bit wary of the other residents.

Several weeks later Sandee and Tesla were introduced to Maggie, a petite woman who had moved in just two days before. The director said that Maggie had neither spoken nor eaten since arriving. Sandee greeted Maggie, inviting her to pet Tesla.

The woman shook her head no.

Sandee smiled at the woman and then followed Tesla around the large room as she said hello to the other residents. After several minutes, Tesla made her way back to Maggie and sat quietly at her feet. At first Maggie seemed oblivious to the dog, whose front left paw rested against her foot. Over the next several minutes, Sandee watched as Maggie put her hand down and touched Tesla's head. Then Maggie leaned over and kissed Tesla. Sandee fought back tears as Maggie began talking to Tesla—telling the dog about a pink dress she sewed for the big dance and how pretty Tesla would look in a pink collar.

Maggie's entire countenance had changed. Her eyes looked brighter, her head was up, and much to Sandee's surprise and delight, Maggie began to sing. The sounds of hymns from long ago filled the multipurpose room, as one by one more and more voices joined in—including Sandee's, whose voice quavered with emotion.

As she sang the chorus to "What a Friend We Have in Jesus," she couldn't help but stare at her dog. Her precious canine girl whose willingness to overlook an offense and meet people where they were had led to a powerful and sacred moment.

What blessings might have been missed had Tesla allowed one negative experience to affect her treatment of the nursing care residents? Have you ever allowed one bad experience to keep you from possible blessings? What role does discernment play in forgiveness and reconciliation?

Paws & Pray

Father, oftentimes it is much easier for me to hold on to a grudge than it is to release it and forgive. You want me to forgive others, just as you have forgiven me. I cannot do this without you. Lord, make me willing to forgive those who have wronged me, and give me insight to understand their actions and discernment to know how to move forward. I know you will help me with each and every step.

Being wise is better than being strong;

yes, knowledge is more important than strength.

PROVERBS 24:5, GNT

28

PROTECTIVE SUGAR

Being wise is better than being strong;
yes, knowledge is more important than strength.

PROVERBS 24:5, GNT

MANY WORDS COULD HAVE BEEN used to describe Sugar: *sweet, self-sufficient, lazy,* and *even-tempered.* The tan and white dog showed up one day for dinner at the Clair family's house and never left.

But the word ten-year-old Gary—the oldest of six children—would have used to describe his favorite dog was *friend.* Gary had found a kindred soul.

The two played together, explored together, and took long walks together.

One day, after a particularly long expedition in a nearby forest, the two of them were relaxing on the porch when Gary's grandma popped her head out the door.

"Gary, I need you to run to the store for me. Here's money and my list."

Gary looked at Sugar. "Are you coming with me?" Sugar flopped onto her side. "Okay, enjoy your nap. I'll see you in a little while."

After walking the few blocks to the store and purchasing the items on his grandma's list, Gary began his short walk home.

"Hey!" a voice shouted.

Gary's stomach clenched as he recognized the voice of his elementary school nemesis, Eddie.

Gary and Eddie had been in the same class each year since kindergarten. And Eddie had made it his mission to pick on, fight with, and generally aggravate Gary every day.

"I'm gonna get you!" Eddie yelled, running toward Gary.

Gary clutched the grocery bags to his chest and started running. He knew he didn't stand a chance against Eddie's fists, but what Gary lacked in strength he made up for in speed.

As Gary got within half a block of his house, he spotted Sugar on the front porch. She hadn't moved.

"Sugar!"

Sugar's normally floppy ears shot straight up, and she leapt from the porch. Suddenly, Sugar was between Gary and Eddie, baring her teeth and growling.

Gary's eyes grew wide. He took a step back from Sugar. He had never seen his dog look so fierce.

"Call off your dog," Eddie squeaked.

Sugar didn't let him say another word. Instead, she started chasing him.

After finding his voice again, Gary called his dog back. To his surprise she obeyed.

"Wow, girl," Gary said, rubbing her back, then sitting down beside her. "That was . . . You were . . . Wow! Thanks."

The next day at school, Eddie stopped Gary in the hall.

"I'm not done with you," he threatened. "You're not always gonna have your dog with you, you know."

Gary thought for a minute, then smiled.

"Maybe not, but now she knows your face and your scent. You'd better remember that."

Apparently Eddie did, because he never bothered Gary again. All thanks to a wise dog who understood that real strength isn't determined by the labels people give you but by the actions you take when it really matters.

PAWS & PONDER . . .

How is wisdom better than strength? Have you ever personally experienced this truth? According to Proverbs 2:6, "the LORD grants wisdom." How are you pursuing wisdom in your life?

Paws & Pray

Lord, sometimes I rely on my own strength in situations instead of asking for your wisdom. You are the author and supplier of wisdom. I want to learn from you how to react wisely, even to defend and protect others if the opportunity arises. Direct me to your Word and teach me how to be wise in all aspects of my life.

29

STOP TIGER!

Watch your tongue and keep your mouth shut,
and you will stay out of trouble.

PROVERBS 21:23

CINDY, A LONGTIME VOLUNTEER at an animal shelter, had just started her shift when the manager asked her to take the short, stocky dog for a walk.

"Of course," Cindy said, grabbing a collar and leash. "I haven't really met Tiger, so it will be a perfect way for us to get acquainted." The shelter was in a strip mall, located not far from railroad tracks. Cindy and Tiger headed to a grassy area in the direction of the train tracks.

Suddenly, the blaring whistle of the train startled both of them, and Tiger began frantically thrashing, backing away from the noise.

Before Cindy could react, Tiger had slipped out of his collar.

Cindy stood frozen, a leash and empty collar dangling from her hand. Tiger stared back at her, not realizing he was free from her control.

"Tiger . . . stay," she said slowly and assertively, attempting not to show her rising panic.

The dog shook his head, then turned around and began running back the way they had come.

"Tiger, stop!" Cindy screamed, trying to close the gap between them. *How can those little legs run so fast?*

"Tiger!" she yelled again.

Miraculously the dog headed right back to the strip mall, but when Tiger reached the entrance of a toy store, the automatic doors opened and he darted right in.

"I am so getting fired," Cindy muttered, following him inside.

Like a drill sergeant, she began shouting orders to everyone she saw.

"There's a loose dog in here. His name is Tiger. Help me get him!"

She pointed to one person. "You! Block that aisle."

Then another. "You! Head over there."

Then she saw Tiger dash around a corner. "Here, Tiger. Come here, boy."

A group of animated children and their parents gathered around her in the aisle. "You distract him, and I'll grab him," Cindy instructed.

Within minutes Cindy had a line of children following her. Great! She could already envision the headlines the next morning: "Hysterical Pied Piper Chases Runaway Dog through Toy Store."

With a roundup crew of store employees, confused parents, and excited children, Cindy made her move. Thankfully, Tiger had worn himself out and had collapsed near the stuffed animals. But as if preparing to wrestle a crocodile, Cindy felt adrenaline take over as she threw herself on top of the overweight, exhausted dog.

"You got him! You got Tiger!" a chorus of children shouted while adults clapped and cheered. Everyone crowded around Tiger and Cindy.

"Thanks, everyone. You were such a big help," Cindy said with a smile as the children got down on the floor by Tiger.

They eagerly petted him, rubbed his belly, and scratched his ears.

After putting Tiger's collar back on and making sure it was securely buckled, Cindy attached the leash and led the heavily panting dog out of the store.

"There you are!" Lisa, the manager of the animal shelter, said as Cindy and Tiger entered the lobby. "I was starting to get worried about you two."

As Cindy filled Lisa in on Tiger's adventurous game of chase, the manager's eyes widened.

"Cindy, did anyone tell you why Tiger was surrendered to us two days ago?"

Cindy shook her head.

"He bit a child."

Cindy stared at her for a moment. She looked from Lisa to the dog to the door she had just walked through.

Cindy sputtered her response, struggling to get any words to come out. "So

*Fear of the L*ORD *is the foundation of wisdom.*

Knowledge of the Holy One results in good judgment.

PROVERBS 9:10

. . . um . . . what you're saying is that I let a child-biting dog into a toy store full of children? And then asked those children to help me catch the dog?"

Not knowing whether to laugh or cry, Cindy was ready to face the music. "I am so fired, aren't I?"

"Well, your adventure with Tiger had a happy and bite-free ending," Lisa said, and both of them burst out laughing with relief.

"You're a volunteer, remember? I can't fire you," Lisa said. "But perhaps it would be best if someone else walks Tiger from now on."

"Absolutely!" Cindy agreed. "Tiger, it was nice to meet you, but let's never do this again, okay?"

The two women laughed all the way to Tiger's kennel. His great adventure ended with him curling up in the corner and falling fast asleep.

PAWS & PONDER . . .

Thankfully, Tiger kept his mouth shut while he was in the toy store. And while most people don't bite others with their teeth, our mouths can still wound others. Have you ever gotten into trouble because of something you said? How might things have turned out differently if you had kept your mouth shut? The next time you feel yourself tempted to blurt out something you know you shouldn't, run your words by God first and ask him if you should say them.

Paws & Pray

Lord, my words can get me into so much trouble. Help me not only to think before I speak, but also to think of you before I speak. Bring to mind any hurtful words I've said recently so that I can confess them to you and be forgiven. And help me to speak words that will make a difference in someone's life.

WISE SNOOPY

There is precious treasure and oil in the dwelling of the wise,

but a foolish man swallows it up.

PROVERBS 21:20, NASB

SNOOPY AND WOODSTOCK, two-year-old boxers, looked very much alike, yet acted very differently.

Snoopy, whose black muzzle distinguished him from his white-muzzled brother, was rarely without a stuffed toy in his mouth. He loved his toys and was surprisingly gentle with each one.

That was not true for Woodstock.

It seemed as though Woodstock's mission was to destroy every toy he was given. Within minutes of receiving a new plush toy, Woodstock would rip it open and begin frantically pulling out the insides. Soon, the floor would be covered in white fuzz.

Meanwhile Snoopy would gingerly carry his new toy around—being careful to avoid his brother, who was still eviscerating his.

What amused Adam and Lisa, the duo's owners, was how Woodstock—without fail—would finish gutting his toy and then run to Snoopy, wanting his. Snoopy would give a warning growl to his brother and turn away, keeping his fully intact toy safe in his mouth.

Woodstock would often whine and yip for several minutes before returning to his shredded toy.

One evening after tearing apart a toy donut and then unsuccessfully trying to convince Snoopy to share his, Woodstock picked up a scrap of his flat donut and lay beside Snoopy.

Lisa couldn't help but laugh at the scene in front of her. One dog held a

135

donut stuffy in his mouth while also guarding two other stuffed toys under his belly, and the other lay in the middle of a pile of fuzz, holding the remnants of a toy in his teeth.

"Oh, Woody," Lisa teased. "When are you gonna learn?"

Woodstock raised an eyebrow as she began to clean up the mess.

She had a feeling that look meant *never*!

PAWS & PONDER...

In what ways do you tend to "swallow up" your treasures? Is this Proverb referring only to monetary treasures? What other kinds of treasure might apply? What are some practical ways you can guard yourself against insisting on instant gratification or using up the resources God gives you?

_____   _____

Paws & Pray

Lord, guide me to know how and when to use the resources you have given me. Give me strength to gather and save my treasures. Father, I want to save wisely, be more generous, and honor you with what you have entrusted to me.

If you become wise,

you will be the one to benefit.

31

ALWAYS CLOSE BESIDE

A friend is always loyal,
and a brother is born to help in time of need.

PROVERBS 17:17

STEPHANIE WAS AT THE HEIGHT of awkwardness—twelve and shy, with a mouth full of braces—when she met Maggie. The preteen was desperately in need of a friend, and the little ball of black, white, and gray fur was ready to be one.

At nine weeks old, Maggie was barely big enough to climb up stairs, but the border collie–cattle dog mix puppy had a loving heart that would grow even bigger as she did.

Maggie sat beside Stephanie at breakfast every morning, and she greeted her best friend with vigorous tail wagging after school. When Stephanie was frustrated to tears with her math homework, Maggie would put her head on her young friend's lap. When the girls at school had a party and Stephanie wasn't invited, Maggie didn't mind Stephanie's tight hugs. When Stephanie wasn't asked to prom, Maggie offered the best antidote: her quiet presence. She was constant, steady, and eager to offer unconditional love, even when the rest of Stephanie's world felt unpredictable.

Their bond increased over the years. Finally, Stephanie graduated from high school and was accepted at an out-of-state college. The days of summer quickly slipped by, and soon it was time to begin packing for school. Stephanie not only wrestled with what to bring, but with deeper questions.

"Will I have any friends? Will I do well in my classes? Will my faith survive in this new environment? Oh, Maggie, will you forget about me?"

There is a friend who sticks closer than a brother.

PROVERBS 18:24, NIV

When Maggie heard her name, she got up from where she was lying and sat attentively next to her friend.

Stephanie's eyes blurred with tears as she took folded clothes off the bed and arranged them in the suitcase, unsure what she would need for this new phase in her life. Maggie watched her pack, her ears slung low and her tail uncharacteristically still. She knew what suitcases meant: goodbye.

Stephanie kept packing, but strangely, she seemed to make hardly any progress. As many items as she put in the suitcase, it appeared as empty as ever. She took a break to eat a snack and talk to her mom. When she returned, there was no denying it: Nearly everything was gone from her suitcase.

Staring at her luggage, Stephanie noticed something out of the corner of her eye—a familiar head nosing inside one of her other bags. Sure enough, Maggie was taking the items out, one by one. The look in her big brown eyes seemed to say, *If you don't pack your bags, you don't have to leave, right?*

"Come here, sweet Maggie." Stephanie buried her head in Maggie's ruff and let the tears fall unchecked. This was precisely what she needed in that moment: a reminder that her dog loved her, her family loved her, and God loved her.

As she looked into her dog's smiling face, a friend with an endless capacity for loyalty and unconditional love, Stephanie believed Maggie was giving her a tiny glimpse into what the friendship of God looked like.

PAWS & PONDER...

What does the phrase "friendship of God" mean to you? Do you consider God your friend? Who in your life points you to the kindness, loyalty, and love of God? Who can you encourage in that same way today?

Paws & Pray

Lord, thank you for the gift of friendship—both with other humans and with animals. You are the perfect example of friendship and love. Help me to follow your example and love others well today and always. And help me be a friend who points others to you.

32

RETIRED JUDGE

Whoever tends a fig tree will eat its fruit,
and he who guards his master will be honored.

PROVERBS 27:18, ESV

BRANDON COX HAD BEEN WORKING as a K9 officer for close to a decade and knew it would take awhile for him and his family to get used to his new role as sergeant. But he was most concerned with how his K9 partner, Judge, would handle the transition. Once Brandon started his new job, their assignments in the field would end.

Judge had been working with the Hernando County sheriff's office in Florida for seven years—and had been working with Brandon the entire time. The dog lived and breathed his work because to the German shepherd it wasn't work at all. It was all one big game. A game he absolutely loved.

The K9 partner was a mass of energy on patrol. He was always on alert and ready to be called into action.

In fact, Judge would often get so excited while on duty that he would bark incessantly during his twelve-hour shift in the cruiser. While the barking was less than ideal in such close quarters, Brandon realized it helped Judge stay focused and ready to work at a moment's notice by providing an outlet for his pent-up energy. Thankfully, Brandon was able to quiet Judge when necessary.

Whenever it was time for Judge to get to work—whether that meant apprehending a suspect, finding a missing person, sniffing out an illegal substance, or putting himself in harm's way to protect his handler—Brandon knew his dog was ready.

Judge was simply always ready.

That quality made him a wonderful partner, but it also worried Brandon now. Would his highly trained police dog adapt well to being a house pet?

Judge was housed at Brandon's home in an outside kennel to keep him used to the elements so he could do his job well in any kind of climate. One of the perks of his retirement would be getting to move *inside* Brandon's house, where he would enjoy a comfortable climate-controlled environment. And yet, as happy as Brandon was to have his faithful partner become a member of his family, he couldn't help but wonder how the dog would respond to the dramatic changes.

Brandon had a hard time imagining Judge lying around the house all day. Would he even enjoy it? But with Brandon's new role, and Judge's age, the decision was made to retire Judge and bring in a younger dog to take his place.

The first week Judge did seem quite confused. He would pant with excitement as Brandon dressed for work, then whine and paw at the door when Brandon left without him. But it did not take long for Judge to embrace a life of ease . . . and air-conditioning in Florida.

Judge traded games like chase the suspect for games of fetch and hide-and-seek with Brandon's children. And he happily traded his kennel in the back of the police car for his soft memory foam bed.

Although his former partner is enjoying the good life of retirement, Brandon knows that if the need ever arose, Judge would not hesitate to serve, defend, and protect him and his family.

Because, after all, he's Judge.

PAWS & PONDER...

This proverb refers to the benefits of hard work. What are some of its rewards? Can you think of any eternal rewards of hard work? What are the "fig trees" (i.e., roles and responsibilities) God has given you to cultivate and nurture? How are you working hard at tending those?

Paws & Pray

Father, help me to work well for you. Show me how to work wisely—not for the praise of others, nor for mere financial gain, but as a testimony to my faith in you. Help me always to work with you in mind. As I work in your presence, allow others to see you in me. For you are my greatest reward.

Too much honey is bad for you,
and so is trying to win too much praise.

PROVERBS 25:27, GNT

33

RUDY, SHAKE

Too much honey is bad for you,
and so is trying to win too much praise.

PROVERBS 25:27, GNT

"MAKE A WISH, LIAM," ANDREA SAID, holding her son's PAW Patrol–themed cake. "And then you can blow out your candles."

Her little boy's face beamed with joy as he huffed and puffed, blowing out each candle one at a time.

"I'm four, Mama!" he said proudly, holding up three fingers.

Setting the cake down, Andrea kissed his head and showed him how to hold up four fingers.

"I'm four!" he repeated, showing the proper number of fingers to his friends who had come to celebrate with him.

The group of ten, six boys and four girls, talked loudly, their mouths full of blue and white cake. The topic of conversation revolved around dogs, both fictional and real.

After each one declared their favorite PAW Patrol dog, they took turns talking about their own dogs, or lack thereof.

"I don't have a dog," Claire said, her bottom lip sticking out in a perfect pout.

"You can pet Rudy," Liam said, pointing to his dog who sat in rapt attention beside him. Rudy was eyeing every bite of cake Liam put in his mouth.

As Andrea walked into the kitchen to put away the trays of chicken nuggets and fruit, she heard Liam add, "Rudy can do lots of tricks. Watch. Rudy, shake!"

Cheering erupted from the dining room.

"Rudy is in doggie heaven," she chuckled, knowing how much their pound pup adored attention.

Ever since they had brought him home from the SPCA, he had lived for their praise. If you weren't paying attention to the forty-pound dog, he would paw, jump, or bark to get you focused on him. It was both endearing and annoying—especially when Liam was napping.

"Rudy, shake!" another little voice commanded.

"Shake me, Rudy!" came another.

A round of giggles and squeals were followed by more commands to shake, sit, lie down, and dance!

Andrea laughed.

"I'm not sure Rudy knows the dance command, guys," she said, walking back into the dining room.

She came to an abrupt halt. Rudy's face, whiskers, nose, the tips of his ears, and his foot were decorated with blue splotches. *Is Rudy morphing into a Smurf?* Andrea wondered. The answer quickly became apparent as she watched a little hand reach down to shake Rudy's paw, before rewarding the dog with a piece of cake.

A reward Rudy was ecstatic to receive over and over again.

"Oh, Rudy," Andrea said with a sigh. "What a mess you are. And how sick you are surely going to be. It's time for you to leave the party."

Rudy was less than pleased when Andrea escorted him out of the room.

Of course, later than evening, Andrea was less than pleased to have to clean up the aftereffects of Rudy's impromptu trick demonstration.

"You just couldn't say no to the attention . . . or the cake, could ya, boy?"

PAWS & PONDER . . .

Too much of a good thing. How can trying to earn too much praise be bad for you? What do you risk when you allow the praise and attention of others to become the driving force of your life? Is there an area in your life right now where you are trying to please others more than God? Would you take a moment to confess that to the Lord?

Paws & Pray

Lord, how easy it is to seek the praise and attention of others above all else, even making myself sick in the process. Forgive me for being more concerned with what others say about me than with what you say about me. Help me to be content with who I am in you.

Smiling faces make you happy,

and good news makes you feel better.

PROVERBS 15:30, GNT

34

REESE'S MISSION

Smiling faces make you happy,
and good news makes you feel better.

PROVERBS 15:30, GNT

HAVING LIVED WITH CHRONIC ILLNESS as a teenager and young adult, Lauren was more closely acquainted with bad news than she cared to be. In fact, there had been seasons of her life when it felt like bad news was the only kind she received. A disappointing test result and frightening prognosis, having to let go of ideas and hopes for the future, and adjusting to her body's limitations all brought a deep sense of loss and grief—for both Lauren and her husband, Alex.

Yet the young couple fought hard to view each hurdle as an opportunity to press into what God had for them. Some of those opportunities had included making career changes, relocating, and establishing a nonprofit ministry called She Found Joy. Through speaking events, devotions, and podcasts, Lauren and her team encouraged women to discover and pursue authentic joy in each and every season.

Even with Lauren and Alex's determination and earnest faith in God, the days—and nights—could still be painful. And choosing joy, or even finding a reason to smile, could sometimes feel like an insurmountable task.

That's when their dog, Reese, a Cavalier King Charles spaniel, shone the most. Ever since he was a puppy, he seemed to have made it his life's mission to give his humans a reason to smile.

With his floppy ears, tan and white silky coat, large inquisitive eyes, and perpetual smile, Reese had come hardwired to make people grin—especially Lauren.

On days when Lauren couldn't get out of bed, Reese was content to snuggle close to her, occasionally lifting his happy little Cavalier face to hers for a kiss. On days when Alex was weighed down by stress at work, Reese gave him a reason to get up and go for a walk to clear his head. And on days when the couple worried about the future or had to absorb difficult news, Reese bounded toward them with a ball, inviting them to lay their worries down for a moment in favor of a rousing game of fetch.

But perhaps the biggest blessing Reese gave Lauren was pointing her to God—her healer and the source of her strength and hope. For while some days were difficult, Lauren has seen better days and knows the best is only yet to come.

PAWS & PONDER...

What brings a smile to your face? What in your life points you to God or causes you to reflect on him? How could you encourage someone to look to God for strength and joy?

Paws & Pray

Father, life can be so difficult. Happiness and joy seem so far away. Please remind me who you are and who I am in you. May I never forget how much you love me. That truth alone fills me with great joy.

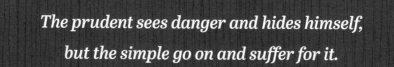

The prudent sees danger and hides himself,

but the simple go on and suffer for it.

PROVERBS 27:12, ESV

35

THE STENCH OF REJECTION

The prudent sees danger and hides himself,

but the simple go on and suffer for it.

PROVERBS 27:12, ESV

"SMOKEY! No!" Tara yelled frantically, trying to rein in the retractable leash. "Leave it. Stop. Sit. Stay. Come!"

Her dog ignored the staccato commands and forged ahead toward his goal—a black and white animal nosing around some bushes. Even though it was dark, Tara could make out the telltale stripe. But her attempts at reeling in her strong hound mix were useless. He was straining against the leash like a sled dog on track to win the Iditarod single-handedly.

"The skunk is not your friend!" Tara explained. "He doesn't want to have anything to do with you. He would rather spray than play."

It wasn't like Smokey hadn't been down this odorous road before. He had been sprayed three times in the past year. Each time, Tara was certain he had learned his lesson.

Normally, she loved Smokey's tenacity. After all, it was his grit that saved his life after being so horribly abused as a puppy. His will to live and determination to survive were evident the first time Tara met him at the animal shelter and fell instantly in love with him. And yet, right now, she really wished he would dial his determination down a few notches.

"Smokey, let me tell you again. That skunk does not want to be your friend. He hasn't wanted to be a friend all year. Come on. Let's get . . ." Too late. The skunk suddenly stopped, lifted its tail, and took aim.

Smokey jumped back. He sneezed and shook his head. Then he ran back to Tara, dejected and confused. His expression broke her heart, and the pungent

smell wafting from him stung her eyes. Tara covered her nose and mouth and muffled, "Bath time for you, mister. Thankfully, I still have a full bottle of Skunk-Off shampoo at home."

Actually, she had three full bottles. After all, you can never have enough neutralizing shampoo when you live in an area where cranky skunks abound.

"Oh, buddy," she said, resisting the urge to pet her dog. "When are you gonna learn that Mr. Stink Spray will never be your playmate?"

Smokey cast a pitiful look toward the bushes where the skunk had disappeared. He then looked up at Tara.

"I know, I know. How humiliating, especially when your intentions were good and noble." She tugged on his leash. "Come on. Let's go home and wash away the stench of rejection."

PAWS & PONDER...

There are times when temptation seems unavoidable—it just seems to come out of nowhere. But other times, as today's proverb describes, you see temptation coming and have a chance to get away. Can you recall a time when temptation suddenly appeared? What about a time when you clearly saw it coming? What temptations do you struggle with most? What are some safeguards you can put in place today to avoid the stench of sin?

——————————————— ❀ ———————————————

Paws & Pray

Lord, thank you for always making a way for me either to stand against or run from temptation. Forgive me when I fail, when I pursue sin, knowing full well the consequences. Enable me to recognize temptation when it is coming my way. And give me the strength to run and hide. Help me to see you as bigger than any sin and any temptation. And help me to trust you far more than I trust myself.

36

WHERE'S BEAR?

The simple believe anything,
but the prudent give thought to their steps.

PROVERBS 14:15, NIV

JODY BELIEVED HER DOG, MOLLY, a two-year-old border collie–Lab mix, was the smartest dog she had ever had. Molly had earned top honors when she completed puppy school and had quickly moved up the obedience school ladder, earning a Canine Good Citizen certificate well before her first birthday.

Molly had an impressive list of tricks she would run through whenever Jody's friends stopped by. And most impressive to Jody, Molly knew her left from her right and could find a specific toy when asked.

Molly's advanced intelligence amazed Jody. But it also amused her.

Jody had learned from Molly that you could be ridiculously smart and still be incredibly gullible.

Molly adored her best friend Bear—a big, gentle three-year-old Rottweiler who lived next door. The two were together almost every day. Any time Molly heard someone say Bear's name, she would run to the back door in anticipation of playing with her friend—regardless of the time of day or if she had just come in from seeing Bear.

Jody's kids used the "Bear card" when Molly had one of their socks in her mouth and they wanted her to let go.

"Where's Bear?" they would ask excitedly. And without fail, Molly would drop the sock in one of the kids' hands before racing toward the back door.

Jody used the "Bear card" when she was trying to get work done at home and Molly started barking.

And Jody's husband used the "Bear card" when he wanted to enjoy a bowl of ice cream without Molly drooling all over his feet . . . because he found it amusing.

Sometimes Molly's humans felt a little guilty for tricking their dog, but she didn't seem to mind.

After all, she may have been gullible, but she was smart enough to know that one of those times the back door would open and she would get to romp with Bear.

Wait! Did someone say Bear?

PAWS & PONDER...

What are the dangers of gullibility? Have you ever trusted the wrong person? What was the result? What role does discernment play in taking others at their word? What steps do you need to ponder today?

❆

Paws & Pray

God, you are most trustworthy and good. Grant me the discernment I need to navigate relationships. Enable me, by your Spirit, to know who I can trust and who I cannot. Teach me to be a trustworthy person so I can point others to you.

An intelligent heart acquires knowledge,
and the ear of the wise seeks knowledge.

PROVERBS 18:15, ESV

37

TRYING TO HOLD IT ALL TOGETHER

Hatred stirs up strife,
but love covers all offenses.

PROVERBS 10:12, ESV

SHARON WAS BARELY HOLDING it together. Her fingers tingled and her mind was fuzzy. She had no idea she was breathing too fast. All she knew was a snowstorm was headed their way, her newborn son had given up sleeping, and her husband's plane was due to land in an hour. Oh, and there was no food in the house.

Trying to clear her throat from whatever felt lodged in it, Sharon fought against her panic. The Weather Channel droned on the television in the background, taunting her for her lack of preparations. But who could prepare for anything with an infant who refused to sleep!

And why did her husband have to be out of town on a business trip this week?

Sure, his boss had told him he had to go, but one look around the messy house and at her reflection in the hallway mirror and she suspected that he had been relieved to leave for a few days. *I wish I could spend a few nights by myself at a hotel,* she thought, then immediately felt guilty for wanting to be away from her baby.

All she had ever wanted was to be a mom. But she had no idea it would be so hard. Or involve such little sleep.

Buster, their yellow Lab, came bounding up to Sharon. "No, Buster," she shouted, startling her son who had just dozed off in the swing.

Buster dropped his ball at Sharon's feet, bumped his head against her leg, and barked expectantly. Sharon screamed at Buster as she picked up his slobbery ball and threw it as hard as she could, knocking over a lamp.

The dog backed away. The baby started to cry. And Sharon sank to the kitchen floor and wept.

As she sat with her hands covering her eyes, her son's cries began to subside. Sharon peeked through two fingers.

Buster was standing by the infant swing. The baby's eyes were fixed on the dog. Buster turned his head toward Sharon.

"Oh, Buster," she sobbed. "I am so sorry."

Her Lab, who didn't know the meaning of holding a grudge, walked over to Sharon and put his head on her shoulder. Sharon held on to the strong dog as she let every fear and anxiety rise to the surface.

With her son sound asleep in the swing, Sharon put on her coat and took Buster outside to play catch.

Minutes later her husband texted to say his plane had landed, and he was going to stop by the store on his way home.

Sharon's anxiety immediately began to dissipate when she read those words.

This time when Buster dropped his ball at her feet, Sharon kissed his head before tossing the toy.

"My steady, loving, forgiving, and slobbery Buster," she cooed. "What would I do without you?"

PAWS & PONDER...

Why do you think fear and anxiety cause a person to act out in anger and hate? Why can responding in love sometimes feel so difficult? Are you facing a difficult situation today? Ask God to show you how to respond in love.

Paws & Pray

Lord, you are love. Whenever I want to react angrily, please help me to stop and think before I say or do anything. Then give me the words to respond to others in love—in person, on the phone, on social media. Father, I need your discernment to know how to respond lovingly to difficult situations that arise, even today.

38

CHATTY ROCKY

The heartfelt counsel of a friend is as sweet as perfume and incense.

PROVERBS 27:9

WITH FOURTEEN HORSES, one miniature donkey, five goats, twenty chickens, and two dogs to feed each day, Jodi Stuber's morning starts early. But she doesn't mind. In fact, she cherishes the quiet time before HopeWell Ranch—the equine therapy ranch she and her husband, Ty, run on their ten-acre property in Weidman, Michigan—is bustling with activity.

Each morning as she feeds the animals, she prays over them, over the people and families they serve, and over the volunteers and supporters who give so generously of their time and resources to make it all happen. It has become a sweet time for her to talk to her heavenly Father—and for her beloved German shepherd, Rocky, to "talk" to her.

From the day Jodi and Ty welcomed Rocky into their home, he joined Jodi on her chores, quickly learning the layout of the ranch and the feeding schedule. In fact, Rocky learned the routine so well that he started herding Jodi from paddock to paddock, letting her know with a variety of verbal sounds that she needed to keep moving.

At first Rocky's canine murmurings were simply an amusing diversion to Jodi during her morning chores. But as time went on and the ranch began serving more people—people hurting and struggling with a variety of difficulties—Jodi found herself having conversations with Rocky as if he were a trusted confidant. Jodi would share her fears and triumphs, her concerns and plans, and her dreams and vision. And as if understanding each word, Rocky would answer with a throaty rumble or a staccato bark.

There were days when Jodi felt too burdened to talk because she was worried about a veteran struggling to find peace, was preparing to host a group of bereaved children whose classmate had died suddenly, or was weighed down by the never-ending financial needs of the ranch. On those days, Rocky would be silent, sensing Jodi needed his presence more than his "words."

When Jodi was brimming with energy and thinking two steps ahead, Rocky listened to her process out loud, responded with an enthusiastic bark, and kept her focused on the task at hand.

Of course, from time to time, Jodi got to play the role of faithful and loyal companion for Rocky. Some mornings her canine friend would walk up to her and lean against her legs—his subtle ninety-pound way of asking for her attention. Jodi was always happy to oblige, kneeling down and inviting Rocky to lay his large head in her hands. As she looked into his eyes and stroked the soft fur between his ears, she said, "Rocky, I'm so grateful for you. You are one of God's gifts to me."

Rocky didn't say a thing—hearing Jodi's words was more important than speaking any of his own.

During those times, with her dog's head in her hands, Jodi could almost hear her heavenly Father whispering his own words of love over her and over all of HopeWell.

PAWS & PONDER...

Who do you turn to when you need to talk things over? Or seek advice? What makes a friend's thoughtful and earnest counsel such a sweet gift? How can you offer that gift to someone today?

_____   ❀   _____

Paws & Pray

Lord, thank you for being my most trusted confidant, loyal friend, and wonderful counselor. And thank you for the friends you have placed in my life who give me heartfelt counsel and who always point me to you. Help me to be a good friend to others, and grant me wisdom to know when to speak and when to simply be present with anyone who is hurting.

*The name of the L*ORD *is a strong tower;*

the righteous man runs into it and is safe.

PROVERBS 18:10, ESV

39

REMEMBER YOUR PACK

Know the state of your flocks,
and put your heart into caring for your herds.

PROVERBS 27:23

WITH HER HEAD HIGH and tail swaying, Penny, a two-year-old Golden retriever, appeared quite pleased with herself as she led the way home. After twenty minutes of jockeying for position with the dogs in her neighborhood walking group, Penny had finally taken the lead—courtesy of an intoxicating aroma at the base of a mailbox, which the other four dogs could not resist. Taking advantage of their distraction, Penny sprinted forward, pulling her owner, Tracy, with her.

"Penny, slow down," Tracy said laughingly, gripping the leash with both hands and running to keep up.

But Penny would not relent. She was determination on four paws.

The rest of the group chuckled as Penny dragged Tracy farther and farther ahead of the group.

Penny didn't turn back. She didn't stop. She was on a mission to stay in the lead. And she did.

Not once did she pause to smell the grass, pick up a stick, or mark where she had been. While the other dogs played among themselves, and their humans enjoyed the first cool front of the year, Penny kept her gaze straight ahead.

Eventually, whether from fatigue or an abundance of confidence, Penny slowed her pace. Tracy took the opportunity to catch her breath and snap a photo of her dog, who was now walking with a distinct swagger.

Tracy knew the photo would be a hit on social media. She typed up a quick caption and hit *share*.

But her joy was short-lived. While Penny stopped to sniff a patch of weeds, Tracy quickly scrolled through the posts on her phone. As she read all the things that others had proudly posted and shared, she was overcome with feelings of failure.

Why can't *I* plan a week's worth of menus for my family?

When was the last time *I* went to the gym?

How does everyone else seem to have it all together?

Then, as if a mental avalanche had been triggered, every item on her ever-expanding to-do list came rushing into her consciousness—a work deadline, costumes to pick up for her kids, a plethora of unread emails in her in-box.

"Ugh, why did I come out today?" Tracy lamented. "I am going to be so far behind."

As Tracy contemplated abandoning the group and running home to try to salvage the rest of her day, she was pulled out of her thoughts when Penny abruptly wheeled around. She braced her front legs against the asphalt and raised her ears in surprise. Penny seemed genuinely shocked to find the others there.

In her determination to get ahead, she had forgotten about those behind.

Melinda, one of the neighbors walking that day, noticed Penny's reaction.

"Penny, when you are leading, you can't forget about your pack," she gently chided the dog.

Melinda's words were meant to tease Penny, but they felt like a lifeline to Tracy. A way to escape the avalanche of to-dos. An anchor in the flood of her feelings of inadequacy.

Tracy did have things to do, but nothing needed to be completed that very moment. Right now, she was part of a pack—a pack committed to encouraging and supporting one another.

Tracy tugged on Penny's leash to get her to take a few steps back. It was all the encouragement the gregarious dog needed to reunite with her friends.

As Penny and her best friend, Layla, leapt toward each other like two polar bears hugging, Tracy tucked her phone into her pocket.

"So, Melinda," she asked the woman walking next to her, whose sister was facing a cancer scare. "How's your sister? And how are you holding up?"

It felt so good to focus on her pack.

PAWS & PONDER...

Who is your pack? Are you walking with them? Or charging ahead? In what areas of your life might you need to slow down and remember those who want to walk with you? What is one thing you can do today to remind yourself to slow down and to care for those you are fighting so hard to lead?

_____ 🐾 _____

Paws & Pray

Father, it is easy to forget about those around me—even when those around me are family and friends. Would you help me to lead from a place of compassion and rest? Help me to know when to push hard and when to fall back. And as you call me to lead, help me remember and care for those who follow.

Many will say they are loyal friends,
but who can find one who is truly reliable?

PROVERBS 20:6

A PICTURE OF LOYALTY

Many will say they are loyal friends,
but who can find one who is truly reliable?

PROVERBS 20:6

LOYALTY CAN BE REVEALED in a variety of ways—a friend defending another, an employer keeping his word, a faithful spouse. But to Cindy and her daughter, Abbey, loyalty looks like a white bichon frise named Baci.

When Abbey, the third of four children, was in elementary school, she was diagnosed with abdominal migraines, a painful condition that led to chronic vomiting every few days—often in the wee hours of the morning. Each night when Cindy heard her daughter heading for the bathroom, she jumped out of bed to join her, not wanting her to suffer alone. Baci always followed close behind.

As Cindy would hold her daughter's hair and rub her back, Baci would curl up on the floor beside the little girl. When the episode was over—usually thirty minutes later—Abbey, Cindy, and Baci would wearily climb back into their beds.

Eventually, the nightly routine began taking a toll, not just on Abbey but on Cindy as well. Her nightly vigils had resulted in extreme fatigue and exhaustion.

One night, Cindy slept through Abbey's nightly run to the bathroom. When she awoke the next morning, she was consumed with guilt.

"Oh, Abbey, honey, I am so sorry I wasn't there for you," she apologized over breakfast.

Abbey's sweet smile warmed Cindy's heart. "It's okay, Mommy. Baci was with me."

Cindy's expression gave away her disbelief because Abbey nodded and added, "Baci followed me into the bathroom and lay down next to me till I was all done."

Cindy picked up the fluffy little hero and gave her a kiss of gratitude on the head.

It wasn't the only night Baci was there for Abbey when she was sick. In fact, it happened numerous times over the next few months.

On more than one occasion, when Cindy did wake up and would start running toward the bathroom, she would be met by a sleepy Baci heading back to her dog bed, after seeing Abbey safely back to her human bed.

Baci had already handled it.

Baci's actions and her unwavering loyalty were a comfort to a sick girl and her exhausted mother—keeping one from feeling alone, while allowing the other to get the rest her body desperately needed.

Thankfully now, ten years later, those sleepless nights and abdominal migraines are a distant memory. And sweet Baci is still providing companionship and loyalty to her most grateful family.

PAWS & PONDER...

What does loyalty look like to you? Who is your most loyal friend? How can you show loyalty to a friend today?

Paws & Pray

God, you have given me so many examples of what loyalty looks like. I see instances of loyalty throughout your Word, in my relationships, and even in the animals I love. And yet, there is no one as loyal as you. I marvel at your steadfast love for me. Help me to look for ways to demonstrate your loyalty and love to others. And enable me to be a truly loyal friend.

41

RASCAL AND BELLE

When calamity comes, the wicked are brought down,
but even in death the righteous seek refuge in God.

PROVERBS 14:32, NIV

WHEN JODI AND DEAN brought Belle home from the humane society and Dean opened the car door, the forty-pound hound mix dashed out, ran across the front yard, and disappeared down the street. For the next hour the couple tried everything to entice Belle back into their yard, never losing sight of her as she darted into neighboring yards. But nothing seemed to work.

Then Jodi had an idea. "I'll go get Rascal. Maybe she will want to meet him."

Their eighty-pound boxer-dalmatian mix was not a search dog, but he did catch Belle's scent immediately in the front yard where she had run. His tail began to wag as he looked around in excitement.

But where is she? Rascal seemed to pose the question as his ears stood up and his head tilted.

Just then, Jodi spotted Belle peeking through a shrub just beyond their property line.

"He is pretty handsome, don't you think, Belle? I know he'd like to meet you."

Deciding to capitalize on Belle's curiosity, Jodi took Rascal into the house and then came back out to help Dean. Rascal's barks of protest could be heard outside—eventually drawing Belle out of hiding. Timidly, Belle walked forward, her eyes fixed on the front door of the house where Jodi was standing close by. Dean was several feet behind Belle, trying not to crowd her.

Jodi and Dean smiled at each other before Jodi opened the door. The two dogs met on the threshold and instantly became best friends as Belle ran inside and grabbed one of Rascal's toys. Rascal didn't mind at all.

"I think this is going to work just fine," Jodi said with relief.

Rascal and Belle played with the same toys, romped together in the same backyard, and slept on the same large dog bed. However, Belle drew the line at eating from the same dog dish and made it quite clear her food was hers alone.

Aside from that one unwavering caveat, the two were closer than any dogs Jodi had ever known. The first time Rascal left Belle for his annual checkup at the vet clinic, Belle whined, cried, and refused to eat or drink until Rascal came home. Several months later, when Rascal needed to return to the clinic for a skin condition, Jodi feared how Belle would react.

After loading Rascal into the car, Jodi—thinking it would be easier on Belle if she were confined to a small area—went to secure her in the laundry room. However, Belle was nowhere to be found.

"Belle, come! Where are you hiding?"

Jodi headed outside, stopping to check on Rascal. He was happily sitting in the back seat of the car, with the door open, just as Jodi had left him. And there, in the driver's seat, was Belle, looking like an eager chauffeur.

If he's going, I'm going, she seemed to say.

Rascal and Belle were never separated again.

On spring days, they would spend hours outdoors watching the neighborhood bloom with new life. On wintry days, Belle would use her nose to plow a path in the snow around the house for her and Rascal. And when Jodi and Dean brought a baby home, Rascal and Belle took turns lying under the crib to guard their tiny human named Lili.

No matter what the days brought, Jodi knew Rascal and Belle would face it together.

Still, when Rascal's health began to decline, Jodi was surprised when Belle's did too. After several months of vet visits and medical care, it was evident that the bonded canines' pain was increasing. Jodi and Dean called the vet in tears to say they were ready to free their dogs from their debilitating pain. To make it less stressful, the vet came to their house. Jodi and Dean got down on the floor, with Jodi holding Rascal on her lap and Dean holding Belle on his, the two friends nose to nose until they took their final breaths.

As Jodi and Dean hugged each other and wept, they knew they weren't facing this loss alone. They had a refuge in God and in each other—a powerful lesson they had learned from two very special dogs.

PAWS & PONDER...

What calamities or troubles are you facing today? Where or in whom are you seeking refuge? God is referred to numerous times in the Bible as our refuge and strength. What makes God such a powerful refuge for us in times of trouble? How can you be sheltered by God in the midst of your troubles and fears?

Paws & Pray

Lord, you are my strength, my shelter, and my hope. You are my refuge in the midst of the storms I face. Help me stay close to you. And help me lead others to the refuge and love only you can provide.

Wisdom is good for the soul.

Get wisdom and you have a bright future.

42

HOT DOG!

My child, eat honey; it is good. And just as honey from the comb is sweet on your tongue, you may be sure that wisdom is good for the soul. Get wisdom and you have a bright future.

PROVERBS 24:13-14, GNT

TEN-YEAR-OLD LIBBY placed five little white cones a foot apart in a straight line. At the end of the line she stacked bricks several feet apart and laid a broom across them. Finally, she laid her old Barbie Pop-up n' Play tunnel at a ninety-degree angle to the broom.

"Perfect!" she proclaimed, running into the house to retrieve her dog, Daisy, and a red cup filled with diced hot dogs.

Using masking tape to attach the red cup to her belt, Libby was finally ready to begin Daisy's agility training. And with the smell of hot dogs in the air, the little white Havanese was more than ready!

Daisy bounced with excitement as Libby attached her pink leash to Daisy's collar and led her out the door.

Libby couldn't wait to teach Daisy how to do the agility course she had set up. After watching an agility show on Animal Planet, Libby had been inspired to create one of her own. And although Daisy had never even been to obedience school, Libby just knew her dog could be the best agility dog in the world.

The energetic little dog yipped and jumped, trying to reach the cup of hot dogs dangling from the waistband of Libby's shorts.

"You gotta earn your treats, girl," Libby explained. "First, I'll walk you through the course. And each time you do something right, I'll give ya a piece of hot dog. Soon you'll be able to do the course without me having to show you. Okay?"

As if understanding the instructions perfectly, Daisy barked and sat at attention.

"Good girl," Libby laughed, giving the dog her first meaty morsel.

Holding Daisy's leash up high, Libby began to walk Daisy in and out of the cones, giving her a treat at every zig and zag. She then built up enough speed to jump over the broomstick. Libby was so thrilled by Daisy's flawless jump that she gave her a handful of hot dog pieces. Libby crawled through the tunnel first, then went back and carried Daisy through. Although she hadn't gone through on her own accord, Daisy was still rewarded with a treat for her trouble.

Libby and Daisy went through the obstacles at least two dozen times, with one break for Libby to refill the hot dog cup.

After an hour, Libby ran inside to ask her family to come out and watch Daisy—the world's greatest agility dog—complete the course all by herself.

Libby watched with pride as her little dog zigzagged around the cones, leapt over the broom, and scurried through the tunnel before running straight to Libby to receive a handful of meat.

Libby's dad laughed as Daisy sank to the ground, head between her paws, belly spreading out beneath her.

"Well, Libby girl, you did it!" he said proudly. "You taught Daisy how to do an agility course." Then he added with a chuckle, "And what a meat coma feels like! How many hot dogs did you feed that dog anyway?"

Libby grinned coyly, shrugging her shoulders. "As many as it took for her to learn."

PAWS & PONDER...

In what ways is wisdom good for the soul? How have you found this to be true in your own life? How does Proverbs 9:12 (see devotion 10) relate to Proverbs 24:13-14? Where does wisdom begin?

Paws & Pray

Lord, I long to be a person who is known for godly wisdom, wisdom that begins and ends with you. Help me to crave you and your Word more than anything else. Make your Word tastier to my heart than honey—or even hot dogs!

A wise woman builds her home,

but a foolish woman tears it down with her own hands.

43

ANNIE'S NEW BED

A wise woman builds her home,
but a foolish woman tears it down with her own hands.

PROVERBS 14:1

GREG AND MEGAN were taken aback when they walked into their central Florida home. The floors of the kitchen and family room were covered in what looked like mounds of snow.

"Um . . . is that—" Megan began, stopping herself before asking the question. There was no way it had snowed inside their house, in the middle of summer, in Florida.

Greg grabbed a handful of the soft white substance.

"Annie," he called. "Come here."

Greg and Megan's seven-year-old corgi emerged from the back bedroom of their ranch-style home. She walked tentatively, as if she were stepping on egg-shells, with her head nearly touching the floor and her tail drooping behind her.

"Annie, what did you do?" Megan asked.

The couple quickly began taking inventory.

The sofa was still intact.

The pillows were all in place.

Their master-bedroom door was still shut.

And Annie's toy bin was filled only with tennis balls and rubber toys. She wasn't allowed to have any stuffed toys because she always destroyed them. Every time Megan was tempted to buy a cute stuffed toy, Greg would tell her she might as well just hand the dog the cash and let her eat the money instead.

What had Annie destroyed?

"In here," Greg called from the back bedroom.

There, in the middle of the floor, were the shredded remnants of Annie's brand-new dog bed. It had been an expensive orthopedic bed Megan had purchased after Annie's last checkup when the vet mentioned his concern about Annie's stiff joints. The vet had recommended a supplement and a quality supportive bed.

Last night was the first time Annie had slept on the bed. And Megan felt confident the splurge was worth it.

Until now.

"Ugh, Annie! That bed was supposed to help you feel better," Megan groaned. "And it was *so* expensive . . ."

Megan and Greg cleaned up the debris before turning in for the night.

Days later, when Annie started limping after playing at the park, Megan went to the pet store to buy another, less expensive bed.

Annie slept all night on the memory foam bed.

She napped on it the next day.

After the third day without a shredding incident, Megan told Greg, "I think we have a winner!"

Until she came home that evening to more piles of foam.

"Oh, my word, Annie," Megan said. "Why do you insist on destroying your beds? I'm only trying to make you comfortable."

As Megan filled the trash with chunks of foam, her mind began to race, searching for solutions. *Do they make dog beds from Kevlar? Can you coat one in Teflon? How can I teach Annie to stop chewing her bed so she can enjoy its long-term benefits?*

Just then, Annie came bounding around the corner—a chunk of foam held firmly between her teeth. Clearly wanting to play with her new "toy," Annie play-bowed to Megan.

"Oh, Annie," Megan chuckled, grabbing a treat from the counter and trading the morsel for the foam. "Maybe I should see if dog beds come wrapped in chain mail!"

PAWS & PONDER...

In what ways might a foolish woman tear down her house? Why do you think the phrase "with her own hands" was included in the proverb? In what ways does a wise woman build her house? What else might the term *house* mean in the verse? How can you guard yourself against tearing down your house with your own hands?

―――――――――――――――――――   🐾   ―――――――――――――――――――

Paws & Pray

Lord, so often I choose temporary pleasure over long-lasting benefits or eternal rewards. I get so caught up running after the things of this world that I forget you are the only one who can truly satisfy the deepest longing of my heart. God, fill my mind with an awareness of you so that I can be strong when I am tempted.

44

A FIERCE LOVE

Don't turn your back on wisdom, for she will protect you.
Love her, and she will guard you.

PROVERBS 4:6

VICKY BELIEVED SHE HAD HIT the proverbial jackpot when she adopted nine-week-old Misty from the SPCA. Even at such a young age, it seemed as if the shepherd mix was so grateful to have been given a home that she was determined to be the best-behaved dog around. And she was.

Misty never had an accident inside the house, never chewed anything other than her own toys, and barked only when she needed to go out or to alert Vicky that someone was at the door. Misty truly seemed like the ideal dog. Some of Vicky's friends were mildly annoyed that their dogs did not have such pristine reputations.

Misty's ideal status only increased after Vicky and her husband, Rick, welcomed two sons into their family a year apart. Misty didn't seem to mind sharing Vicky and Rick's attention. Instead, she delighted in the presence of two more humans to love. She often slept in the same room with the boys, lay beside them on the floor when they played, and sat in the kitchen with them while they ate.

Misty was a fierce and loyal companion—something Vicky was grateful for the day a man knocked on the door.

After securing her two-year-old in his high chair, Vicky answered the door with her one-year-old in her arms. Misty followed Vicky to the door, then sat off to the side, just out of the man's view.

The man said he was selling cleaning products and wanted to give Vicky a demonstration. Vicky pointed to the child in her arms and laughed. "I'm sorry. I have my hands full at the moment. Thanks, but I'm not interested."

The man persisted, however, continuing to talk about the product and urging her to give him a few minutes of her time. Vicky became annoyed and went to close the door, but the man grabbed the door and attempted to jerk it open. As he did, Misty charged from her position, leapt past Vicky, and released a menacing growl. Vicky had never heard such a sound come from her dog. Misty chased the man down the sidewalk, the cleaning supplies dropping from his hands as he took off running. Vicky allowed Misty to get several houses away before she called her to come back. Vicky saw no trace of the man after that, and he never returned for his cleaning supplies.

Vicky has no idea what might have happened that day, but thanks to Misty she doesn't need to worry about it. Misty was there to protect her family—a family she fiercely loved. And a family who fiercely loved her right back.

PAWS & PONDER...

How does wisdom protect you? How does wisdom guard you? What does it mean to protect and love wisdom? What are practical ways you can do that? How has wisdom protected you in the past?

_____   ❀   _____

Paws & Pray

God, thank you for the gift of wisdom. Help me never to turn my back on your gift but to cherish and protect it. Allow wisdom to guard my life so that others will see you in me.

*The eyes of the L*ORD *are everywhere,*

keeping watch on the wicked and the good.

45

WHEN YOUR DOG TALKS . . . LISTEN

A person finds joy in giving an apt reply—
and how good is a timely word!

PROVERBS 15:23, NIV

JEN WAS FULL OF NERVOUS ENERGY about her dad's upcoming open-heart surgery. Questions swirled through her mind. Would everything go smoothly? How extensive would his rehab be? Would there be long-term consequences? *I need to find something to take my mind off Dad for a little while*, she thought. She opened the pantry and saw the plastic bin that contained all of the teaching supplies she had been using for the past four years with her preschool class at church. The bin had reached its capacity and then some. It was time to cull the contents. She began pulling out finger puppets, construction paper, and Popsicle stick signs that quickly littered the floor.

She swallowed the worry lodged in her throat. Her fingers grew cold with fear.

I am not going to start down the what-ifs trail, she thought as she stuffed a handful of ripped paper plates into a trash bag.

Her cell phone rang. It was her mom.

The trash bag slipped from Jen's hand.

Thankfully, her mom was just calling to confirm Jen's flight information. Jen moved into the kitchen to make herself a cup of tea while she continued the conversation. When she hung up, Jen noticed her hands were shaking.

Once again, she tried to swallow her fear.

What if?

She scrubbed the dishes in the sink.

What if?

She began rearranging the boxes in the pantry.

She heard her dog, Bailey, walk into the kitchen, but Jen was far too busy trying to avoid thinking about her dad to pay the fluffy Golden retriever much attention.

With the pantry done, Jen closed the door. She was scanning the kitchen for something else to tackle when she came to a complete stop.

Bailey was holding one of the signs from Jen's bin in her mouth: a bright orange sign with the word "Pray" written on it.

Of all the things in the bin. Of all the signs—happy face signs and sad face signs, "green means go" signs and "red means stop" signs, giant ear signs to remind the kids to listen, and big eye signs to remind them to pay attention—Bailey had picked the "Pray" sign.

Jen dropped to her knees in front of her dog and wrapped her arms tightly around Bailey. She began to sob, something she should have done days ago when she first learned of her dad's diagnosis.

And then, after gently taking the sign out of Bailey's mouth, Jen did what her dog suggested—she prayed.

And as she prayed, she felt fear begin to loosen its grip on her heart.

Bailey stayed with Jen the entire time she prayed on the kitchen floor. Jen prayed for strength and peace, healing and protection, joy and mercy. Then she spent time praising God and thanking him for her parents, her dad's doctors, and her friends and family who were helping in so many ways. Above all, she thanked God for loving her so much that he sent her a message through her dog.

A dog who had given her just the right word at just the right moment.

PAWS & PONDER...

Can you recall a time someone shared a timely word with you? How did that word help you? Is there someone in your life today who might need a word of encouragement? How could you speak words of life, grace, and hope to that person today?

Paws & Pray

Lord, thank you for speaking to me through your Word and through the words you give others to say to me. Give me the courage to speak words of life to those around me. Open my eyes to see the needs of others. And then open my mouth and my hands so that I might help to meet their needs as much as possible.

Pride brings a person low,

but the lowly in spirit gain honor.

PROVERBS 29:23, NIV

PUTTING HER FOOT DOWN

Pride brings a person low,
but the lowly in spirit gain honor.

PROVERBS 29:23, NIV

FOR EIGHT YEARS, GRETCHEN, a miniature smooth-haired black and brown dachshund, enjoyed her status as the sole animal in her family's household. With two adults and seven children, she always had someone giving her attention, playing with her, and accompanying her on outdoor adventures across acres of rural Colorado property.

However, one day things changed dramatically. Everything started out normally until a truck with a large trailer backed into the driveway. The kids seemed excited about something. And then a ramp came down behind the trailer and the door opened. Gretchen took a few steps back as the largest animal she had ever seen was coaxed out.

"It's okay, Gretchen," one of the kids assured her. "It's a gentle quarter horse." But all the dachshund saw was a creature that towered over her, smelled different, and made funny noises. Who invited this interloper to live with them?

She barked her displeasure loudly.

"Gretchen, quiet! You'll spook him."

The small dog had other plans.

For weeks, she grabbed every opportunity to bark at the horse, prowled around him while he ate, stole his treats, nipped at his hooves, and occasionally rolled in his manure.

"Eww, Gretchen! You stink. Stay away from the manure piles."

No one but Gretchen understood the reasoning behind her behavior.

She didn't care that her family wasn't pleased with her. She had a message to communicate.

After several months, Gretchen finally settled down. Clearly the horse was staying, but Gretchen seemed to feel that the horse now understood where he stood on the hierarchy of her humans' affections—at the bottom.

Gretchen was once again enjoying her queen bee status on the couch in the house when she heard another truck with a trailer backing up in the driveway. She sprang to her feet and rushed to the window, just in time to see an even larger interloper emerging from the trailer.

No!

When one of the kids opened the back door, Gretchen raced out, straight to the pasture. Now there were two tall-legged, attention-stealing intruders inside the fence. Gretchen gave them a piece of her mind.

"Be nice, Gretchen," the oldest boy warned her.

Gretchen barked louder. She crouched as if preparing to pounce on the new horse. And then she ran under the fence railing into the pasture where her barking, stalking, nipping, treat stealing, and manure-rolling antics began again.

Several weeks later, the teenage brothers were busy building a hay shed under Gretchen's watchful eye. Things seemed to be progressing well, so she made her way to the pasture to remind the horses who was boss.

Suddenly, there was a terrifying sound—half squeal, half cry. The five brothers stopped nailing shingles on the roof of the shed and looked toward the pasture.

The Arabian mare was standing in front of the hay box, with her front hoof on Gretchen's back.

The little dachshund was sprawled out with her belly flat against the ground. The mare slowly turned her head toward the dog. No one moved.

"Is Gretchen dead?" one brother whispered.

They each feared the answer.

But then, the mare lifted her hoof and Gretchen shot up like a rocket before bolting out of the corral as fast as she could.

The perceptive horse had decided to put her foot—or rather her hoof—down on Gretchen's bully-like behavior. Not to crush her, or to hurt her in the slightest bit, but to calmly and powerfully communicate that it was time for her to stop.

After that day, Gretchen decided the horses could have the pasture. She would be content to enjoy her own privileges of being allowed in a warm house, sleeping in her people's laps, and held closely in their hearts.

PAWS & PONDER...

What are some ways you have seen pride bring a person low? Conversely, can you think of an example of how someone has received honor as a result of their humility? What are some areas of your life in which you struggle with pride? Confess them to the Lord, and ask him to give you a heart of humility and compassion for others.

Paws & Pray

Lord, I often think of myself far more than I think of others. Please be quick to convict me of my prideful thoughts and replace them with your thoughts. Lord, help me to follow your example of humility and compassion.

47

A SECRET MELODY

No one who gossips can be trusted with a secret,
but you can put confidence in someone who is trustworthy.

PROVERBS 11:13, GNT

THE MOMENT KELLY saw her eleven-year-old daughter Mia, she knew something was wrong. Her normally happy-go-lucky girl trudged through the pickup line with drooped shoulders and downcast eyes. When she got into the car, Mia silently buckled her seat belt, folded her arms tightly around her middle, and let her head drop forward in defeat.

Mia's posture reminded Kelly why no amount of money would ever entice her to relive the middle-school years.

Change, she thought. *So many changes happen all at once.* As if changing classes, changing bodies, and changing hormones weren't enough to make even the happiest of children grumpy, the stress of changing friendships and learning (often the hard way) whom you could count on was enough to make every kid wish they could fast-forward through middle school.

So far, the most painful lesson for Mia was finding someone she could trust.

When Mia began to cry in the car, the story came out. Thinking her sixth-grade secrets—her crush on a classmate and her dream of being a princess at Disney World—were safe with the friends she had trusted since third grade, she had shared them. Her so-called friends had blabbed her confidences to the entire lunch table.

"I will never trust anyone again!" she vowed as they arrived home.

Inside the house, Melody, their four-year-old Golden-collie mix, came bounding toward them. Mia dropped her backpack on the floor and ran into the family room. Kelly knelt down to pet Melody.

"I think someone needs a friend, Mellie," Kelly whispered.

Melody followed Kelly into the family room where Mia was lying facedown on the sofa, a pillow over her head. Kelly sat down beside her daughter and began to rub her back. Melody put her head right beside Mia's. Her black nose pressed against Mia's wet cheek, and she began to lick the salty tears.

A small hand moved and gently touched Melody's side.

Kelly smiled.

"You know," Kelly said, "Melody is really good at keeping secrets."

Mia gave a muffled response. "That's because she can't talk."

"Exactly," Kelly said. "That's what makes her such an excellent secret keeper. After all, she's never told you any of my secrets, has she?"

Mia slipped the pillow under her head and turned over to look at her mother, switching hands to keep petting Melody.

"You tell Melody secrets?" Mia asked incredulously. "But you're a married grown-up! You don't have any secrets."

Kelly nearly choked on a laugh.

"Sure I do," she said. "Big ones too."

"Like what?" Mia asked skeptically.

Kelly hesitated before answering, lost in her own thoughts. *It's true. There are some things that I have never shared with anyone except Melody—and God.*

"Well, one secret I've told Melody that I'll share with you—because I know I can trust you—is that I'm scared of talking in front of people."

Mia sat up.

"But you talk in front of people all the time. It's part of your job."

Kelly grinned. "I know, but the truth is, I'm terrified every time I do it."

"Mama, can you tell me another one of your secrets?"

Kelly thought for a minute. "Want to know my biggest secret?"

Mia nodded.

"Deep down in my heart, I still feel like I'm in middle school and worried about what everyone thinks of me."

Mia laughed. "For real?"

The righteous choose their friends carefully.

"For real," Kelly admitted.

Mia scooted closer to Melody. "And Mellie helps you? Like when you talk to her?"

It was Kelly's turn to nod. "She sure does. Mellie always listens, even to my silliest fears and secrets. And I never ever have to worry about her laughing at me or telling anybody what I said. She really is man's—or rather, woman's—best friend."

Mia slid onto the floor next to Melody. "Do you mind if I talk to Melody for a little bit?"

Kelly kissed the top of Mia's head. "I don't mind at all. I'll leave the two of you alone." But just before leaving the room, Kelly turned around and looked lovingly at her daughter.

"Just remember. I'm pretty good at keeping secrets too."

A bright smile lit up Mia's face. "I know, Mama."

"Thank you, God," Kelly prayed out loud as she walked into the kitchen to start dinner. "Between you and Melody, I think we all just might survive the middle-school years."

PAWS & PONDER...

Have you ever been betrayed by someone you thought you could trust? Did it affect your willingness to trust others? Do you have a trusted confidant? Are you a confidant for someone else? Why is trust so important in relationships?

Paws & Pray

Father, no one is more trustworthy than you. Thank you for the dear friends and animals you've given me who remind me I can trust you—at all times. Help me to be a treasured and trustworthy friend to others.

48

A ROSE FOR FELICIA

A person's spirit can endure sickness,
but who can survive a broken spirit?

PROVERBS 18:14, CSB

FELICIA TRIED TO TAKE a deep breath to settle her nerves. But the breath caught in her throat as pain from her recent lung surgery radiated across her chest.

It had been only five days since the lobectomy. Doctors had removed three-quarters of her left lung in order to stop the cancer that had metastasized to this part of her body.

Felicia's world had turned upside down five years earlier when she was diagnosed with stage 3 colon cancer. She had endured major surgery, thirty-eight rounds of radiation, and twelve rounds of chemo that first year, and at the end of it all, her doctors pronounced her cancer-free. But just before celebrating the all-important five-year-cancer-free milestone, Felicia learned that the cancer had returned.

She was devastated by the news, yet she knew she needed to fight just as much this time. But the brutal battle was taking a toll on her body and her mind.

Now Felicia began to withdraw. Her own body had turned on her. Nothing felt safe anymore.

She had a deep faith in God and knew he was with her, yet the fear, doubt, and pain were relentless.

Felicia tried again to slow her breathing and calm her mind. She adjusted the pillows propped up behind her and began to cry out to God—for help, for hope, for strength.

Hours later, after the pain had subsided and the fear had retreated, she was overcome with the strongest desire for . . . a puppy.

What a ridiculous idea! Who gets a puppy while fighting cancer and recovering from major surgery? she argued with herself.

But day after day and week after week, the desire grew stronger. Felicia began searching online for puppies. She visited animal shelter websites, pet message boards, and Facebook breeder groups. She even sent her son to check out some possible candidates.

Just to give him something to do other than worry about me, she said to herself.

And then a friend sent her a photo of a black Lab puppy who needed a home. *This* is *my new dog*, Felicia thought.

Her son was surprised at the choice. "I thought you wanted a small fluffy dog who would lie on the bed and snuggle with you. This puppy is going to grow into a large, active dog. Are you certain you want this one?"

"Yes. And I've already decided to call her Rose."

Rose was no wallflower—she was a bull in a china shop who was always on the go and into everything. And the sweet bundle of energy was exactly what Felicia needed.

Instead of lying around wondering what the future held, Felicia needed to get up and feed Rose. Instead of wallowing in despair and worry, Felicia needed to take Rose outside. And instead of withdrawing from those around her, Felicia socialized with Rose and played with her.

Felicia moved slowly, but she moved. And she healed.

Felicia still had moments of fear and doubt, but then Rose would give her a sloppy kiss on the face and place a paw on her leg. And Felicia was once again smiling. God still had a plan and a purpose for Felicia's life, with Rose by her side.

PAWS & PONDER . . .

What has threatened to break your spirit? Where did you turn for help? For hope? If we believe in him, God promises each one of us a future and a hope. In what ways does knowing God loves you, that he is for you, and that he is your hope help sustain your spirit?

Paws & Pray

Lord, life can feel so hard sometimes. My spirit can feel so defeated and overwhelmed. Father, draw my heart ever closer to yours. Whisper your name over me, reminding me of who you are and who I am to you. And as you fill me with hope, help me to share that hope with others.

A RUDE AWAKENING

It is dangerous to have zeal without knowledge,
and the one who acts hastily makes poor choices.

PROVERBS 19:2, NET

OVER THE YEARS Jan and Paul's dogs had acquired quite a rap sheet with the local police department. The black Labs, Jack and Piper, loved escaping the confines of their fenced-in yard—only to run straight to the police station less than a mile away and turn themselves in.

The Labs' escapades were the topic of many conversations—and quite a few laughs—among Jan and Paul's family, friends, and colleagues.

But sadly, just a few years after his first run-in with local law enforcement, Jack passed away.

And as if desperate to find her best friend, Piper became obsessed with escaping.

Piper had always had a talent for finding any and all weak spots along the fence line, but after losing Jack she became single-minded in searching for other ways to get through the wooden barrier.

Piper would find some loose slats and push herself through or shimmy her body through a small gap in the gate.

Keeping an eye on Piper had become a constant battle.

One morning, several months after losing Jack, Jan got up before sunrise to attend an early-morning Bible study. Not wanting to disturb her husband or Piper, who was sleeping in the hallway just outside their room, Jan quietly snuck out of the house, locking the front door of their hundred-year-old farmhouse behind her.

Unbeknownst to Jan, Piper decided to follow. Maybe she wanted to go with

Jan, search for Jack, or just enjoy the sunrise. That morning, Piper added another trick to her skill set: pawing at the handle on the front door until the lock disengaged, and the door popped open. At least, that's what Jan and Paul would surmise.

Not long after Jan left for Bible study, a neighbor called the police, concerned that Jan and Paul's front door was wide open and their dog was wandering around the front yard.

Two police officers arrived quickly and found everything as the neighbor described.

The officers cautiously entered the house with Piper following close behind.

The officers searched the house and eventually came to Jan and Paul's bedroom—where Paul was still sound asleep!

"Sir? Sir!" shouted the officer standing closest to Paul. He shined his flashlight in Paul's eyes. "Sir! Are you okay?"

Paul sat straight up in bed, startled awake. He tried to make sense of the scene before him.

Why are the police in my room?

Where is Jan?

Why are they asking if I'm okay?

So many questions.

And one very affectionate dog licking the officer's hand.

Piper. *Of course.*

After assuring the officers he was fine, Paul quickly grabbed his robe and saw the officers to the door.

An hour later Jan returned home.

"Janis!" she heard Paul bellow as she walked in the door. "You left the front door ajar. You are never going to believe what *your* dog did!"

Jan protested her innocence. "What did Piper do this time?"

As Paul recounted his early-morning police welfare check and wake-up call, Jan could barely keep from laughing.

After hearing the story, Jan got ready for work, and on her way out, she made sure the door was securely closed behind her. She hadn't been at the office long before the phone rang. It was Paul.

"Piper escaped again—on her own. I'm sorry I blamed you. We'll both need to take extra measures."

From that day on, Jan and Paul made sure the front door was closed and bolted when they left the house, much to Piper's dismay.

PAWS & PONDER...

Have you ever made a poor choice because of a hasty decision? What was the result? Can you think of a current example of someone exhibiting zeal without knowledge? How might haste cause problems for yourself and others? How can you guard against making hasty decisions?

Paws & Pray

Lord, help me to think before I act. Direct my thoughts to you—who you are, what you have done, and what you would have me do. Help me pause to pray, consult your Word, and seek counsel from others so that I do not act rashly and regret it later.

50

A WALLET-SIZE
TREASURE

The hopes of the godly result in happiness.

PROVERBS 10:28

"BEAUTIFUL."

Phil and Bonne turned around in their booth at the family pet expo and saw two women standing in the aisle, both with big smiles.

"My mom loves dogs," the younger woman explained. "Especially terriers. We had Lakeland terriers when I was growing up. But it would be difficult for Mom to have a dog now."

"Well, let me tell you about our dogs, Flurry and Finna," Phil said. "They are from Ireland . . . in case our decorations didn't give you a clue." The eight-by-eight area included an array of shamrocks, an orange-green-and-white covering on the table representing the colors of the country's flag, and a laminated map.

"The breed originated in the Wicklow Mountains and was used as spit-turning dogs and badger hunters. They almost became extinct during World War II, and while their numbers are slowly growing, they are still considered a rare breed. Currently, there are only a few hundred in the world."

"It's why we decided to do an informational booth here," Bonne joined in. "To give people a chance to see this wonderful breed in person."

The older woman was kneeling down now, catching Finna's attention. The wheaten-colored Glen seized the opportunity to plant her front paws on the visitor's legs and gave her a series of rapid kisses.

Her daughter watched her mother's face beam with delight. "Oh, yes. Mom really misses that exuberant terrier love."

She tapped her mom on the shoulder, and when her mom looked up, the daughter's fingers began to move as she said, "Mom can't hear. I'm telling her what you told me about your dogs."

The mother's face brightened even more. Then she signed something back to her daughter.

"Would it be okay if I took a picture of your dogs? That's part of the reason we come to the pet expo. Mom enjoys looking at the photographs."

"Of course," Phil said. "Sit nicely, you two." Flurry immediately complied while Finna needed a treat to persuade her. The women stayed and loved on the dogs for a while, then thanked Phil and Bonne before leaving.

The following year the Glen booth was located in the same spot at the expo. The first visitors to arrive were the mother and daughter. Finna and Flurry greeted them warmly, as if to say, "We've missed you. It's been a whole year!" Phil gave the two of them an update. "Finna had a litter last year, and one of her puppies will be in the booth later today. You should definitely come back."

They did come back that year and for several years after, always making a beeline for the Glens.

The sixth year, only the daughter arrived. She sat down quietly and scratched Flurry behind the ears. "My mom died last year, but I had to come and show you something I found among her possessions." She pulled out a small creased photo of Flurry and Finna.

"My mom kept this in her wallet, and as you can see, she pulled it out often. It made her so happy."

Suddenly Finna barked, breaking the poignant moment and demanding attention. Phil, Bonne, and their terrier-loving friend laughed at the feisty intrusion while wiping a few tears away. "Time to make someone else happy."

PAWS & PONDER...

What are you looking toward today to make you happy? In whom, or what, is your deepest hope and greatest longing? How might aligning your hopes with God bring happiness and joy to your heart?

Paws & Pray

God, thank you for everything you've given me that brings me happiness. I know that earthly happiness is fleeting, and you are the source of true and everlasting joy. Fill my heart to overflowing with your joy so others will want it too.

Let love and faithfulness never leave you;

bind them around your neck,

write them on the tablet of your heart.

PROVERBS 3:3, NIV

ABOUT THE AUTHOR

JENNIFER MARSHALL BLEAKLEY is the author of *Joey: How a Blind Rescue Horse Helped Others Learn to See* and *Pawverbs: 100 Inspirations to Delight an Animal Lover's Heart*; a former child and family grief counselor; and a children's curriculum writer. When Jennifer is not typing away on her beat-up computer, you can find her spending time with her talented software engineer/woodworking husband, her two growing children, and her very needy Golden retriever. She and her family live in Raleigh, North Carolina.

ACKNOWLEDGMENTS

THIS BOOK WOULD NOT EXIST without the help of so many kind, generous, and talented people. It truly was a team effort—and I think we make a pretty amazing team!

Thank you to everyone who submitted and shared stories with me. It was a delight to learn about your dogs and to see glimpses of God's grace through the lessons they have taught you—and now me.

Words cannot begin to express my gratitude to my incredible team at Tyndale.

Sarah Atkinson, thank you for hearing the word *Pawverbs* and getting so excited. I am so grateful to you for helping me develop this concept.

Bonne Steffen, you continue to be my superhero. I can never thank you enough for making my stories tighter and better.

Ron Kaufmann, your artistic talent blows me away. Thank you for making this book so beautiful.

Each part of the process—from concept to design to editing and to launch—happened because of the expertise of the entire Tyndale team and made this a dream project for me. I could not be happier with how it turned out. Thank you for allowing me to write about dogs all day!

I am also so grateful to my friends and family who offered encouragement, prayers, support, and understanding during the writing process. You are such a gift!

Darrell, Andrew, and Ella, thank you guys for once again enduring far too much takeout and far too little clean laundry. I love you all so much and couldn't have written this book without you.

Mom, Daddy, and Aunt Judy, thank you for brainstorming with me and helping me remember stories from long ago.

Father God, thank you for the gift of animals. Thank you for revealing glimpses of your heart through the animals you've given us.

And finally, Gracie Jade, thank you for sitting with me as I wrote each story, for hugging me when I felt overwhelmed, and for reminding me to take play breaks. My life is so much richer and covered in dog hair with you in it.

Much love,
Jen

PHOTOGRAPHY CREDITS

2 Jennifer Marshall Bleakley and her Golden retriever, Gracie © 2019 Greenflash Productions Photography

4–5 Dog running on beach © Dmitry Islentev

8 Puppy Suzie Poo courtesy of Amber Palmer

11 Yellow Lab in grass by Vincent van Zalinge/Unsplash

11 and throughout hand drawn line pattern © pashabo

14–15 Basset hound running with branch © Ksenia Raykova

16 Beagle puppy © Sigma S

19 Weimaraner by Freddie Marriage/Unsplash

20 Black pug by Charles Deluvio/Unsplash

23 Pug laying down by JC Gellidon/Unsplash

24 Yellow Lab by Nice Sandhu/Unsplash

27 Bullet the dog with hedgehog toy courtesy of Sarah Atkinson

28–29 Great Pyrenees © Konstantin Tronin

30 Portuguese water dog by Janosch Diggelmann/Unsplash

33 Golden retriever by Cloé Fontaine/Unsplash

34 and back cover Terrier by Hamish Kale/Unsplash

37 Norfolk terrier © Niwiko

38–39 Brown and black dog by Marko Blažević/Unsplash

40 Chocolate Lab © Dustin Hardin

43 Yorkshire terrier by Daria Turchak/Unsplash

46 Maltese © Eric Isselee

49 Maltese close-up © Jolanta Beinarovica

50–51 Greyhound racing © Fotoeventis

52 Australian shepherd dog by Patrik Kopčo/Unsplash

54 Lucy, Australian cattle dog, courtesy of Thom King

58–59 Dog at sunset by Patrick Hendry/Unsplash

60 Happy the Pit bull courtesy of Jacqueline L. Nuñez

63 Dog on guard by David Taffet/Unsplash

64–65 Dog with head out car window © Christin Lola

66 Dog inspecting turtle © Luna Love Photography

69 Dog on gravel road by Tadeusz Lakota/Unsplash

70 English cocker spaniel © Eric Isselee

73 Lakeland terrier by cmophoto.net/Unsplash

74–75 Labrador retriever © Africa Studio

79 Dog with stick in water by Jeremy Perkins/Unsplash

80 Tan dog in field by Cole Wyland/Unsplash

83 Setter in the woods by Ryan Stone/Unsplash

84–85 Dog sitting in the grass by Vincent van Zalinge/Unsplash

86 Brown Lab by Rafael Ishkhanyan/Unsplash

91 Brown and white puppy © Valeria Boltneva/Pexels

92–93 Puppy swimming underwater © Denis Moskvinov

97 Setter in grass by Ryan Stone/Unsplash

98 Shepherd mix puppy by Thomas/Unsplash

101 Shepherd outdoors by Alexandra Richardson/Unsplash

102–103 Terrier with newspaper © Sue McDonald

104 Miniature pinscher on bench © otsphoto

107 Miniature pinscher relaxing © e-Kis

108 Golden retriever holding flag © LightField Studios

111 Black dog close-up by Heather Miller/Unsplash

112 Smiling Goldendoodle by Noah Austin/Unsplash

115 and back cover Manchester the Goldendoodle courtesy of Julie Chen

118–119 Border collie playing © Vera Reva

121 Dog sitting on road by Drew Hays/Unsplash

123 Petting Golden retriever © Jean Alves/Pexels

124 Tan and white dog by Erda Estremera/Unsplash

127 Dog by gate by Annie Spratt/Unsplash

130 Boston terrier by Angelos Michalopoulos/Unsplash

132–133 Scratching a beagle's ears by Leighton Robinson/Unsplash

134 Tan boxer © Mindaugas/Pexels

137 Great Dane © msgrafixx

139 Border collie close-up by Daniel Lincoln/Unsplash

140 Australian shepherd close-up by Tomas Dolezal/Unsplash

142–143 Labradors in lake © dezy

144 Police dog © Africa Studio

147 Dog in snow by fezbot2000/Unsplash

148 Dog shaking hand © Krisana Antharith

151 Beagle eyeing cake © Anneka

152–153 English bulldog lounging © B. Stefanov

154 Cavalier King Charles Spaniel on bed by TR Photography/Unsplash

157 Miniature schnauzer © Lunja

158 Sad dog by Jarrod Reed/Unsplash

160 Puppy in grass by Greg Lippert

162–163 Bulldog with ball by Rodolfo Sanches Carvalho/Unsplash

164 Border collie at sunset by Tadeusz Lakota/Unsplash

167 Rottweiler puppy carrying bowl © Grigorita Ko

170–171 Saint Bernard in snow © Grigorita Ko

172 Shepherd laying down by Niclas Moser/Unsplash

175 German shepherd jumping by Tiim/Unsplash

176–177 Rosie Cotton, a Yorkie/Cairn terrier mix, sleeping with toy courtesy of Nate Rische

178 Dogs with dog walker © Lucky Business

181 Group of dogs sitting by Matt Nelson/Unsplash

182 Bichon Frise by Seth Reese/Unsplash

185 Bichon on leather armchair by Matt Briney/Unsplash

186–187 Brown and white Chihuahua running on beach © cynoclub

188 Boxer Dalmatian mix © SikorskiFotografie/iStockphoto

191 Pointer sitting in grass © nelladel

192 Happy puppy © michaelheim

195 Border collie jumping through agility tire © Flatka

196–197 Dog balancing muffin © Ksenia Raykova

198 Corgi in a café © LoveCorgi

201 Setter sleeping by Ryan Stone/Unsplash

202 Serious dog by Eternal Seconds/Unsplash

205 Shepherd at attention by Michael Dziedzic/Unsplash

206 Dog in armchair by Diana Parkhouse/Unsplash

209 Dog licking snow off nose by Marcus Löfvenberg/Unsplash

210–211 Black Lab stretching © Natalia Fedosova

212 Red longhaired dachshund © Ekaterina Kurakina/Dreamstime.com

215 Smooth coated dachshund in yard by Christen LaCorte/Unsplash

216 Rough-coated collie © Erik Lam

219 Dog in tree by Jamie Street/Unsplash

220–221 Airedale terrier © msgrafixx

225 Black Lab puppy by André Spieker/Unsplash

226 Black Lab by Jadon Barnes/Unsplash

229 Black and white cocker spaniel © Rebecca Ashworth

230 Glen of Imaal terrier © Anna–Mari West

233 Irish Glen of Imaal terrier © Radomir Rezny

234–235 Rottweiler puppy sleeping © Anna Hoychuk

236 Jennifer Marshall Bleakley and her dog, Gracie © 2019 Greenflash Productions Photography

Back cover Dog with ball © Halfpoint/iStockphoto

Back cover Dog catching disk © Ksuksa/iStockphoto

Back cover Puppy running © Bigandt Photography/iStockphoto

Back cover Dog giving paw © soul studio

Back cover Puppy sleeping by Freestocks/Unsplash

Endsheet Cat and dog pawprints © Prikhnenko/Depositphotos

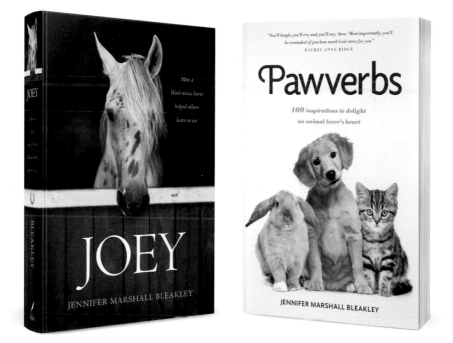